EURO 2004
Fact & Quiz Book

EURO 2004
Fact & Quiz Book

by Lloyd Pettiford

Capella

Published by Arcturus Publishing Limited

For Bookmart Limited
Registered number 2372865
Trading as Bookmart Limited
Blaby Road, Wigston, Leicester LE18 4SE

This edition published 2004

British Library Cataloguing-in-Publication Data: a catalogue
record for this book is available from the British Library

Set in Barmeno by Mike Harrington

Arcturus Publishing Limited
26/27 Bickels Yard, 151–153 Bermondsey Street, London SE1 3HA

ISBN 1-84193-213-2

Printed in Denmark

Contents

Introduction 6

Chapter 1
The Qualifying Campaign 33

Chapter 2
**England's Qualifying Campaign – The Great
Escape Part 2 (or 3)** 76

Chapter 3
The 2004 Championships – The Finalists 103

Chapter 4
The Key Players 185

Introduction

As I write it is the morning after England won the rugby World Cup. I didn't really mean it to happen that way but I have to admit I was very, very drunk indeed. But that is by the by. I only mention it to set the most appropriate tone (i.e. one of sporting triumph) and so you'll know I write with a hangover, so that if you're reading this in the check-out queue and don't know whether to buy it or not, I assure you it will get better once the effects of victory over Australia have receded. Anyway, this is a book which will hopefully turn out to be about another sporting triumph for England. I'm not sure if anything is sweeter than beating Australia in a major sporting final, but I'll wager that victory over France or Germany in the finals of Portugal would come pretty close...

It's actually very nice to be asked to write a book about the European Championships. I get to do all sorts of research and learn lots of useless stats about football – great! My wife already thinks I have too much of my brain devoted to useless sporting trivia, but then what does she know? She thought ringing everyone I knew in Australia when we got in last night was a bad idea – actually, since it was taking me approximately 15 seconds to form each word, she may have had a point...

Anyway, so what is this book about? Well, mostly it's about the qualifying tournament for Portugal 2004 – including a 6-1 play-off humiliation for Scotland – and about the qualifying teams – including England (but not Scotland or Turkey). It's also about the key players for each of those teams and has a special section on England's players and how they got us to the final. There are also quizzes throughout. In conclusion, I offer my predictions for the group matches, quarter- and semi-finalists and finalists and challenge you to beat me.

The story of qualification is often bizarre. Some teams like France and the Czech Republic eased through. Other groups were very tight indeed, including England's. And there were surprises: Greece qualifying ahead of Spain, for instance, was a major shock, although bettered by Latvia's play-off win against Turkey. England's own qualification was odd in the sense that a team that struggled in the second-half of matches at the World Cup finals suddenly became the comeback kings, doing most of their good work in the latter part of matches. The chapter on England's path to the finals is followed up by a more detailed look at the form and players of the teams that qualified, then in the key players section I try to identify not only the established names like Beckham and Ballack, but also those who may emerge in the tournament like Berbatov and Cech.

Before all of that, there are some quizzes on the History of the European Championships. If you don't score too well, don't worry – it's this time which matters, and it might give you some interesting brain-teasers to amaze people with down the pub. I hope you enjoy this book and feel fully armed as a result of reading it to point out more useless facts over the 90 minutes than John Motson. Most of all, I hope it turns out to be a souvenir of England's fine victory! Well, we can dream.

And before that, and to get us in the mood, a look back to our last major success at football. Wouldn't it be nice to forget about 1966 and all that? Not completely, obviously, but if Eng-er-land could only repeat the feat it would be much more exciting than always harking back to past glories. But until then we must reflect upon the glorious year of 1966 – and not only because the author was born then. No, 1966 was also the year that England managed to do what Spain, Portugal, Scotland and a re-united Germany have never managed to do, and 32 years before the French at that. England won the World Cup! And although the European Championships isn't quite the World Cup, it would be nice to win them at least once! But until that happens, here's a look at those heroes of 1966.

In Goal, Gordon Banks (Leicester City)
Pub conversations seeking to identify the greatest England XI of all-time will invariably begin with

'It's gotta be Banksie in goal.'

And although some stupid t***** is likely to add 'but what about Shilton?' they will always and quickly be shouted down in the general consensus that Gordon was great and Banks was brill. When his career was ended by the loss of an eye in a car crash in 1972, the strength of feeling for him was demonstrated as more children sent cards via the TV programme *Blue Peter* to wish him a speedy recovery than ever contributed to the Cambodia 'bring'n' buy' sale appeal or made a pencil holder for dad out of used loo rolls and sticky-backed plastic.

Gordon had modelled himself on Bert Trautmann, the German prisoner of war who had stayed behind after the war and, like it or not, become an ambassador for Germany in the sense that people wondered if the 'Hun' could be all that bad if such a bally hero as Bert was one of them. Banks did a pretty good impression of Bert, although he missed out Trautmann's lunacy of playing with a broken neck. Banks conceded just 0.8 goals a game in his international career. Better still, in World Cup matches Banks let in, on average, less than half a goal a game and even admits to giving himself a really hard time about not saving a penalty from Eusebio in 1966. OK, so his role model Bert saved 60% of the penalty kicks he ever faced but Gordon ought to go easy on himself, Eusebio really was rather good!

In 1972, a little before the car crash, Banks became the Football Writers Association 'Footballer of the Year'. The only previous goalkeeper to win the award was Trautmann in 1956. It was a fitting end to his career, although even without one eye he was still good enough for a couple more seasons in US 'soccer'. But remember, in England's greatest team there's no doubt whatsoever, it's gotta be Banksie in goal.

Full Back, George Cohen (Fulham)
George's proudest moment in life came in 2002 when he got through to the last six of Britain's Brainiest Footballer, hosted by Carol Vorderman. Although the competition was shrouded in controversy – *Guardian*-reading assassin Graham Le Saux refused an invite – George looked to be heading for a final round confrontation with two third division footballers no one has ever heard of until his chances were scuppered by a particularly tricky set of questions on 'The Arts'. Prior to this TV quiz, of course, George's proudest moment came when he was a part of England's winning team in 1966.

As a player George literally had a life-long affair with Fulham FC. Well no, actually, not literally because that would be as silly as David Pleat (or was it Graham Taylor?) opining that an Italian player in Euro 2000 'literally had no left foot'. For George to have literally had a lifelong affair with FFC, he'd have probably had to work his way through Elsie in the tea bar, the girls in the ticket office and today he'd be snuggling up with Al Fayed on a Friday night. So no, not literally an affair with FFC, but he was a one-club man.

Yes that rarest of creatures, a one-club man, the likes of which you don't really find in the modern game, apart from that bloke from Guernsey who played at Southampton. Nowadays Fulham has a range of current internationals

including Dutch and Portuguese, but George was still the most recent Cottager to play for England while with the club. Having won his battle with stomach cancer, George now has to live with the shame of being more stupid (though slightly slimmer) than Alan Brazil, who won 'bronze' in Britain's Brainiest Footballer. Also the only Jewish member of the team and uncle of Ben Cohen, winner of the rugby World Cup in 2003 with England.

Other Full Back, Ray Wilson (Everton)
It may well be that poor old Ray, and not John Connelly, is the least remembered of the 1966 winning team, but he was a fine player. Like Francis Benali (former goalscorer for England Schoolboys), Wilson was once a forward, who tried his luck at full-backing. Fortunately he took to the position like a duck to water, unlike Franny who took to it like a cat to water...but bless him, he does try.

Ray kicked off his England career following military service in Egypt, making his full debut in 1960 away to Scotland. Without national service he might well have earned more than his 63 caps. Mind you, he might also have turned into the kind of ill-mannered guttersnipe who doesn't know the meaning of respect and could really do with a bit of discipline.

Almost missing out on the 1966 finals with a back injury, Ray went on to play a vital part in quarter- and semi-final goals. Whilst not being as famous as Moore and Charlton, both Cohen and Wilson were stalwarts of the defence, who played 28 times together.

1966 was a great year for Wilson, the World Cup being

the second time he'd climbed the Wembley steps, having won the FA Cup 3-2 with Everton against Sheffield Wednesday. He experienced a less happy ascent in 1968 as Everton lost to a Jeff Astle strike and his career went downhill thereafter. After captaining Oldham he joined the family firm of funeral directors. Denis Law described him as the most difficult player he ever had to pass.

Vicious Defensive Stopper Type (Rarely Appreciated) – like John McGovern – But Nonetheless Vital, Nobby Stiles (Manchester United)

Nobby Stiles was born James Alfred Stiles but decided that Jimmy was neither frightening nor silly enough to worry other players. At around 4 ft 7in it is unsurprising that he wanted to be a bit more frightening so he changed his name by deed poll to 'Nutter' B****** Stiles. Alf Ramsey later insisted he change this to 'Nobby'.[*]

In the 1966 group game versus France, Nobby committed the most horrendous of tackles and was booked. Nowadays of course, refereeing inconsistency means a player can be sent off because the ref senses garlic on their breath and yet another time not even be booked for serious offences like attempted murder. However, in those days, Nobby's booking for a scything challenge was thoroughly merited and FA officials put pressure on Ramsey to drop him.

Fortunately, Alf was stubborn and pompous in equal measure and in a Wenger-like show of loyalty insisted that Stiles (vicious animal or not) played in the quarter-final v

[*] None of this opening paragraph is true, of course, and Nobby was a magnificent 5ft 5in when fully erect.

Argentina. Stiles proved a hero as England beat those animals from the Argentine (Ramsey, 1966). In the semi-final Stiles was then charged with kicking lumps out of Eusebio (er, sorry 'marking' him) as England won 2-1.

In the final, Stiles' faith never dimmed as he was convinced England could win. By the end he was so tired that he could hardly move, although somewhat unluckily his last ounces of energy were expended in a silly jig caught for posterity by a camera. To quote a phrase Stiles was a 'son of a bitch but he was our SOB'!

Lanky Centre Half, Jack Charlton (Leeds United)

Although Stiles never became known as 'Small Nob Stiles' for some reason, 6ft 2in Jack did become 'Big Jack Charlton'. In fact he almost became 'Pig Jack Charlton' but the offer of a job with the police arrived just a day after he had already committed himself to Leeds, for whom he made his debut aged 17.

Oddly, he was almost 30 before he won his first England cap and that just a year before the World Cup final. A great sense of timing indeed. Jack went on to prove his shrewdness when he became the first man to spot that almost everyone in the UK was Irish (the author is 1/32nd Irish for instance) but that only some of them were good enough to play for England. But that was later.

Prior to his alchemy in Eire, Big – almost pig – Jack played in all six of England's World Cup games with brother Bobby and afterwards travelled to the council offices in their home town of Ashington to receive a gold watch and engraved tankard. Thus the brothers completed a unique double by both monopolising the north-east memento scene and the Footballer of the Year award (Bobby in 1965/66 and Jack in 1966/67).

Jack also did impressions. His favourite was a giraffe (so called by his team mates because of his telescopic neck) but he also did a 'mini Bert Trautmann' by playing (and scoring) on one occasion against Scotland with a broken toe. According to subtle Alf Ramsey, Jack was only picked because he fitted in with a game plan. Harsh though this seemed at the time, the idea that any old donkey could win with a game plan stuck with Jack when he came to manage the Republic of Ireland. Presumably taking the job because of excellent Irish fishing, Jack's tactics of hoofing the ball into corners and then pressing the throw-in succeeded in producing a desperately dull team of Anglo-Irish who did much better than Eire had ever done before.

The Rather More Elegant-Looking Centre-Half, Bobby Moore (West Ham United)

Robert Frederick Chelsea Moore (that is his real name, this isn't a rehash of the Stiles gag) played 108 times for England, 100 of those under Alf Ramsey. His first game as skipper came when he was just 22 as England thumped the Czechs 4-2 in Bratislava. Although playing in the 1962, 1966 and 1970 finals, Moore didn't play a qualifying round for any of these competitions.

Possibly the most famous of the 1966 team (although Geoff and the Russian linesman come close), Moore also enjoyed club success, helping West Ham to FA Cup glory in 1964 and European Cup Winners Cup success in 1965.

However, a faultless career on the pitch is often remembered also for false accusations of theft whilst on a pre-World Cup (1970) shopping stopover in Bogota, Colombia. The trumped-up charge saw him delayed for four days before joining the rest of the team in Mexico. Latin American prisons are not the best World Cup preparation, but although England were eliminated Moore looked his usual assured self.

Moore returned to Wembley as a Fulham player in 1975, though by then no longer an England player. Unfortunately in the decade of plucky minnows gloriously winning the FA Cup in red and white stripes, Fulham were unable to join in, losing, perhaps inevitably, to West Ham. After a spell in the US and another season with Fulham, Bobby Moore retired after exactly 1000 senior games. He died of cancer on 24 February 1993, aged 51.

Tireless Runner in the Middle of the Park, Alan Ball (Blackpool)

Radio 1 DJs Mark and Lard often pondered and questioned the managerial genius of Ball, none more so than when he took off a lanky centre forward replacing him with a winger, and when he encouraged his team to time waste even though they needed a goal to avoid relegation. 'Squeaky voiced little t*****' I think was how they put it. However, Ball the manager is underestimated; let's face it, not many men have kept Southampton in the Premiership for consecutive seasons, even if the second was while he was managing Manchester City, who edged the Saints on goal difference for the privilege.

But let us instead reflect upon Alan Ball the footballer. Son of a professional footballer, Alan never had any doubt that he wanted to follow in the family business. He was able to fulfill his ambition of playing for England before his 20th birthday by just three days. At age 20 years and 5 days he already had three caps which included a 2-1 win against Sweden.

Alan's triumph is all the more remarkable for the obstacles he has had to overcome. Not just the short, squeaky, ginger ones but also spectacular O level failure. Perhaps this 'lack' in the brain department can explain taking off tall strikers so that the winger you bring on no longer has a target man? But we did say we were going to focus on the player. Coming into the World Cup squad late, Ball played in four of the six games, including the final where his tireless running made all the difference.

Alan played for Bolton as an amateur, Blackpool when winning the World Cup, Everton, Arsenal and Southampton. Whilst with the Gunners he is reputed to have stood on the ball in one game, then jumped off as the defender raced towards him, before knocking it round him. As a manager he retained that level of confidence – and always sent out entertaining teams – but alas his skills were more limited. Ah but who cares, he helped England win the World Cup.

Hat-trick Hero, Geoff Hurst (West Ham)
Geoff Hurst was the adopted son of Davinder and Jetinda Jagpal who found him abandoned in an orphanage in Bombay. He came to England with them in 1946 travelling

third class on a big boat. Once in England, a playground accident led to him having to have his left arm replaced by one carved from solid teak.

No, of course that's not true but then you're really searching for something original to say about the man. His hat-trick in the 1966 final is the only one to have been scored in the final and is included in a total of 24 goals in 49 international caps. Not surprising that this total is lower than that managed by Charlton, Lineker, Greaves, Finney and Lofthouse, but it is also fewer than Robson (the war horse) and Platt (the balding horse).

A good player and crucial to the successful West Ham team of the mid 1960s, Hurst found the ball really ran for him in 1966. Despite the heroics of a goal in the 4-3 win over Scotland at Hampden in only his second international, by the time the World Cup rolled around, Jimmy Greaves had thumped four past Norway and played the first three of England's World Cup matches. However injury to Greaves saw Hurst score the winner against Argentina in the quarter-final and even when Greaves was fit, Hurst kept his place for the final.

Eight months after the final, Hurst scored another hat-trick in a 5-0 drubbing of France. Wow! When will we ever again see our strikers knocking in hat tricks as we put five past top European opposition? As seemed fashionable, after spells with Stoke and West Brom, Hurst tried his hand at soccer in the US. He thought it was all over...and of course it was.

He of the Famous Shot, Bobby Charlton (Manchester United)

The incredible esteem with which Bobby Charlton is held is indicated by Gary Lineker's spot-kick against Brazil which would have equalled Bobby's record of 49 goals for England. Instead of blasting home as he had done so many times before, Gary decided to tap the ball to the keeper in deference to Charlton. How I bet Gary wishes that were true, rather than him having stubbed his infamous toe trying one of those 'great when they go in' chips.

Anyway, Bobby played for Manchester United for 20 years and won the European Cup, League and FA Cup with them, averaging almost one goal in three games. With England he won the World Cup and averaged almost one goal in two games. Sir Matt Busby said of him 'he was as near perfection as man and player as it is possible to be.' He received an OBE and, in 1994, a knighthood. Not a bad career really.

Bobby, as is well known, grew up in the north-east where he lived 'in't shoe-box in middle't road'. Whenever he got the chance he played football, usually with pigs' bladders. Of course much of the time he was being pushed up chimneys, with a chimney fire unfortunately burning all his hair off aged 13. His success, in spite of it all, is surely proof that today's footballers are far too pampered.

Bobby's first England goal came against the might of Scotland, only 10 weeks after he had survived the Munich air disaster in 1958, but he did not get picked for any of England's World Cup games in Sweden, 1958. Going on to play, as he did, in 1962, 1966 and 1970 he can consider

himself unlucky not to have played in four consecutive finals, but then again it was quite a reasonable career anyway.

Nobby Stiles said of Bobby 'He is the greatest player in the world. A wonderful all-round player with the grace of a gazelle – unlike that clumsy giraffe of a brother of his'. Bobby said of Nobby 'Oh my, oh my, he's the greatest dancer, that I've ever see-een'. Jack said of Nobby 'Wait till I get my hands on you, you short a**** little b*****'. Jimmy Greaves said of Bobby that he 'was the perfect foil, with the strength and tenacity of two men. I fed off him for years.' Presumably he then felt thirsty.

Unsung Hero, Roger Hunt (Liverpool)

Of course Graham Taylor's reign as England manager proved that almost anyone could play for England (and Sven has chipped in with a cap for Francis Jeffers), but before such ideas were fashionable, Roger Hunt was perhaps as unlikely a World Cup hero as England had. Don't get me wrong, Roger was a great player, but being turned down by Bury is a less than auspicious start for any career.

In 1959, whilst in the army near Swindon and playing for a local team, both Liverpool and Swindon offered Hunt terms. Amazingly, money-bags Swindon offered better terms, but home-sick Hunt chose tiny Liverpool. When Liverpool won promotion to the top division three years later, Hunt scored 41 times. 1962 was also the year of his England debut, as he scored in a 3-1 victory against Germany's second team, Austria. He was then omitted for 14 games before returning and scoring again in a 2-1 away success against Germany's real second team, the DDR (East Germany). In 1964 he scored four in a demolition of the USA in New York, when unlike 1950, England really did score 10.

In 1966 he scored three goals in six World Cup games and his quick thinking in claiming Hurst's 'goal' rather than trying to put the rebound in to make sure was pure inspiration. His intelligent and unselfish football might find modern day comparison with Teddy Sheringham (though not from me) but Hunt's 245 goals in 401 games for Liverpool is almost beyond comparison in the contemporary game. Despite stepping down from international football in the face of press pressure to recall Jimmy Greaves, Hunt also managed more than one goal in every two internationals (18 in 34). 'Sir Roger' as he was to Liverpool fans, was a very, very nice man.

The Other Forward, Martin Peters (West Ham United)

Martin Peters was a Cockney. To Geordies this means anyone born anywhere south of Yorkshire, but Martin was a real genuine Cockney, being born within the sound of Bow Bells, having a Thames lighter-man as a father and having rather a thing about jellied eels.

At the 1966 World Cup he played five of the six games, replacing John Connelly after the first match against Uruguay. John Connelly, eh? Just goes to show not everyone in the squad was famous!

Martin scored 20 goals in 67 games for England and captained England four times, including the home match v Poland that saw England eliminated from the 1974 World Cup qualifying. Martin's nickname was the ghost, because

of his ability to appear unseen at the far post to head goals. But given Nobby Stiles' opinion that he was impossible to pin down, perhaps 'the eel' would have been more apt?

Not Forgotten, Jimmy Greaves (Tottenham Hotspur)
Martin Peters was said to have been traumatised by the fact that his boyhood hero Greaves was omitted from the final. Would England have won the World Cup if Greaves had played in the final? The fact that we don't know means we probably ought just to be grateful for victory. And of course, along with the 11 who played, Greavsie is, at least, remembered...which is more than can be said for...

Forgotten, John Connelly (No Idea)
John Connelly was in the successful 1965 England team which avenged the 6-3 defeat by Hungary. Connelly was picked for the first match v Uruguay but missed out thereafter. He is included here as a representative of all those nearly men. But then again, he actually played in a World Cup finals and he played for England! Until Graham Taylor's reign devalued that idea, that is something that all those in the crowd would dearly have loved to do...

The Manager, Alf Ramsey
What a pompous big-head! A man of few words, big success and enormous faith in the fact that it had to be 'my way or the high way'. Amongst his most famous few words was his entreaty to his tired players before extra time of the final against West Germany, 'You've won it once, now go out and do it again' he said. And they did.

After a promising start as a player with Southampton, he swapped the path of the good and the righteous for the dark side, represented then, as now, by Spurs. A year later he was a member of the team which beat Scotland to qualify for the 1950 World Cup finals, and at those finals he was a member of the team which lost 1-0 to the United States. Unsurprisingly a man of few words on that particular subject, he was once asked if he had played in the match against the US. He replied that he was the only one who had. There is no independent evidence that he was any better than the rest.

Ramsey was also there, and scored, against Hungary in the famous 6-3 defeat. It was his last international. After thus being involved in the two matches which did most to shatter English football's unreasonable sense of superiority, it was surely only right that Alf sought to rebuild the superiority complex and salvage his own pride by winning the World Cup as manager. Indeed, that England would do so was something Alf confidently predicted when taking the job in 1963.

In May 1965 when England, including John Connelly, beat Hungary 1-0, the team had a familiar look from numbers 1 to 6. Banks, Cohen, Wilson, Stiles, Charlton and Moore. But the 7-11 selected by Ramsey that day Paine, Greaves (who scored), Bridges, Eastham and Connelly – all failed to survive through to the final.

As the finals approached, Ramsey settled upon a 4-3-3 formation which saw the team become known as the Wingless Wonders, the phrase capturing the popular imagination in a way that calling them the 'Fluid system

with a defensive bias in the context of the era, in which any one of several players can fill the "hole" and support the attack' probably couldn't have.

Alf was one of those people of whom it is said he demanded complete loyalty and respect but offered the same in return. Actually, people were probably just rather scared of him. But arrogant Alf or not, you can't argue with the record books.

Trainer, Harold Sheperdson
England's trainer since 1957 under Walter Winterbottom and one of those people with whom Alf established his famous rapport of loyalty and respect. Harold described the 1966 World Cup as his greatest memory; in fact he was so excited that when England won he jumped from his seat and raised his arms in triumph. Understandable, you'd think? Alf told him to 'sit down'.

The Star Linesman, Vladimir
They won't admit it, but it still annoys the Germans...

Historical Quick Quizzes

Historical Quiz 1

1. How did England remain unbeaten in the 1960 European Championships but still fail to win it?

2. How did Spain remain unbeaten in the 1960 European Championships but still fail to win it?

3. Apart from the fact that France lost, what else was good about the 1960 semi-final between France and Yugoslavia?

4. How did the USSR not lose the 1968 semi-final but still not make the final?

5. In the 1972 qualifying campaign, who got most points at the group stage — Finland, Norway, Malta, Republic of Ireland, Luxembourg or Albania?

Answers

1: They did not enter. 2: After winning 7-2 on aggregate v Poland, they refused to travel to the USSR for the quarter-final. 3: The score, 5-4. 4: The game against Italy was decided by the toss of a coin – mind you, so often games *are* decided by tosser's these days, eh Graham? 5: They all got one point each except Albania who managed a 3-0 win against Turkey for two points

Historical Quiz 2

6 Who scored the most goals in 1972 qualifying?

7 Who was the only team to beat Czechoslovakia in the tournament which culminated in the Czech's 1976 penalty victory over Germany?

8 Which was the only home nation's team to qualify for the quarter-finals in 1976?

9 In 1976 qualifying, which was the only Scandinavian nation *not* to finish bottom of their group?

10 True or false? Luxembourg produced their best ever qualifying campaign for 1976 drawing twice against Hungary and beating Austria to amass a mighty total of four points?

11 How many goals did Cyprus score in 1976 qualifying?

12 What was their best result?

Answers

6: England scored 15 in Group 3   **7:** England, who beat them 3-0 in Group 1's first qualifying match   **8:** Wales   **9:** Sweden, but only because they were in the same group as Norway, who did!   **10:** Like b******* did they, but they did rather do well in 1996 in beating one of the eventual finalists.   **11:** Nil   **12:** A 1-0 defeat by England

Historical Quiz 3

(13) In 1980 qualifying, how many points separated the group winners and bottom placed team in Group 6?

(14) Which were the two teams referred to above (top and bottom) and what was the aggregate score of their two games?

(15) The highest score of 1980 qualifying was West Germany 8 Malta 0. But what was the score in Malta?

(16) Who would have qualified for France 1984 instead of Spain if the Spaniards had only won their final group game against Malta 11-1, instead of 12-1?

(17) Who had a 100% winning record in the France 1984 finals?

(18) Which three teams have held the finals twice?

Answers

13: Only two   14: Greece finished top on seven points, with the USSR bottom on five. The aggregate score was USSR 2 Greece 1 with each side winning at home   15: Malta 0 West Germany 0   16: Holland   17: France who won five out of five   18: France in 1960 and 1984, Italy in 1968 and 1980 and Belgium 1972 and – with Holland – 2000

Historical Quiz 4

(19) Which two teams which have held the tournament are very unlikely to hold it again?

(20) When was East Germany's last appearance in a European Championship, 1988 or 1992?

(21) Why was that?

(22) The highest score of 1988 qualifying was England 8 Turkey 0. But what was the score in Turkey?

(23) How many points did England drop in 1988 qualifying?

(24) Why was 1988 qualifying group 6 not like the Eurovision Song Contest?

(25) In 1988 Luxembourg's one point from qualifying group 7 came against who?

Answers

19: Yugoslavia, 1976 and *West* Germany, 1988 – they no longer exist as states. **20:** 1988. **21:** Because by 1992 stage 1 of German plans to dominate Europe were complete in the form of German Unification, 1991 **22:** Turkey 0 England 0 **23:** Just the one – against Turkey **24:** Because although Cyprus got a point it was not from Greece, to whom they lost twice 4-2 at home and 3-1 in Greece **25:** Scotland

Historical Quiz 5

26 Did Scotland finish nearer the top or bottom of qualifying group 7 in 1988?

27 Who had the worst finals records of 1988?

28 As in 1984, in 1992 Spain scored half their qualifying goals in one game. True or false?

29 Having shared joint worst record of the 1988 finals with England, Denmark went on to win 1992 despite initially failing to qualify. Did England fare any better too?

30 So who was worse than England in 1992?

31 Oi, what's the CIS? Sounds like an insurance company to me.

Answers

26: Depends. They finished fourth of five teams, but were eight points ahead of last placed Luxembourg and only two adrift of the top team Ireland. **27:** England and Denmark both lost all their three games, scoring twice and conceding seven. **28:** Technically false. In 1984 they knocked in 12 against Malta to finish with 24 scored. In 1992 they beat Albania 9-0 and scored only 17 in total – so actually just over half. **29:** Oh yes, Graham Taylor's finely honed machine were seventh best of the eight countries taking part. **30:** The CIS **31:** The Commonwealth of Independent States is the name given to the loose association of post-Soviet states before they were quite confident enough to say 'actually we'd prefer our own country please, if you don't mind Boris?'

Historical Quiz 6

32 Once all these post-Soviet types had gone their own way how well did they do in 1996? Azerbaijan for instance?

33 Wasn't this the glorious era of Luxembourgeois football?

34 In 1996 who finished bottom of Group 6 despite drawing away to the table topping Germans?

35 In 1996 which two teams not previously in the tournament finished qualifying with 100% losing records?

36 From which finals group did both 1996 finalists come?

37 True or false? Over half the games at Euro 96 were 0-0 at half time?

38 How many games finished 0-0 at Euro 96?

Answers

32: They scored their only point of 1996 qualifying in a 0-0 draw against Poland and also lost 10-0 to France. It is interesting that Cyprus got their only point in qualifying two tournaments earlier in a 0-0 draw with Poland. Well, when I say interesting... **33:** Indeed it was. 1-0 wins against Malta (twice) and Czech Republic (who only lost in the final on a golden goal) as well as a 0-0 draw against Belarus saw Luxembourg achieve 10 whole points. Still nowhere near qualifying mind... **34:** Wales **35:** San Marino and Estonia **36:** Germany and the Czech Republic were both in Group C. **37:** True, 16 of 31 **38:** Five

Historical Quiz 7

39 Which two teams of Euro 96 were involved in more than one 0-0 draw?

40 Which teams, other than winners Germany, finished the Euro 96 tournament undefeated *except* for penalty shoot-outs?

41 Of the teams which played in the finals of Euro 96, regardless of how many games they played, which conceded the fewest goals?

42 Who then was the only team to breach that impregnable Scottish defence?

43 Who was the only finalist not to score at all at Euro 96?

44 Norway lost just once in Euro 2000 qualifying. When and against whom?

Answers

39: France and Holland, including one against each other. 40: England, France and Spain
41: France, Spain and Scotland all conceded just two   42: England of course in the
memorable 2-0 win at Wembley! 43: Turkey. Must be something about England, eh?
44: Their first game at home to Latvia

INTRODUCTION

Historical Quiz 8

(45) Which goal secured England's path to Euro 2000?

(46) Cypus finished Euro 2000 qualifying with a 50% won/lost record including winning their opening match. In doing so they were the only team to take points off the eventual group winners. Who did Cyprus beat and by what score?

(47) What was the score when Spain met Cyprus in Spain?

(48) In 1996 Azerbaijan got their first European Championship point against Poland. Did they get their first win in 2000 qualifying?

(49) Azerbaijan's only other goal and point came, quite impressively, against who?

(50) Estonia got the hang of it a bit too. Where did they finish in Group 9?

Answers

45: Henrik Larssen's goal against Poland probably had most to do with it **46:** Spain 3-2
47: Spain won 8-0   **48:** Oh yes, they walloped Liechtenstein 4-0 at home. They did lose 2-1
away mind you   **49:** A 1-1 draw against Portugal, who avoided the play-offs by being best
runner-up   **50:** Third behind Scotland and the Czech Republic

31

Historical Quiz 9

51 In all the play-offs the teams were separated by a single goal at most, except for one pairing. Which one?

52 Only one team finished the 2000 finals with a worse record than Germany – who?

53 Who won the 2003 rugby World Cup and what was the score?

54 Jonny Wilkinson of course scored the winning drop goal for England, but who scored the English try?

55 Why was the above victory so deserved?

Answers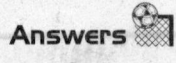

51: Denmark eased past Israel – oh yes, very European – 8-0 (5-0 away)   **52:** Denmark   **53:** England beat Australia 20-17, after extra time   **54:** Ol' Twinkletoes himself, Jason Robinson   **55:** Because I'm fed up with all those whinging Matildas, that's why. They're just miffed because most of them are really English anyway. I've never known such a bunch of ungracious winners *and* ungracious losers. God save *your* gracious queen! All I've got left to say is..."Rolf Harris, Kylie Minogue, Bob Hawke, Pauline Hansen, Lleyton Hewitt, David Campese, Harry Kewell, Mark Viduka, Skippy the bloody bush kangeroo, INXS, and especially Russell bloody Crowe – your boys took one hell of a beating! Your boys took one hell of a beating!

Chapter 1

The Qualifying Campaign

Introduction

It's amazing when looking back on a qualifying campaign that so many results and goals which seemed irrelevant at the time turn out to be highly significant. Similarly, matches which seem to be important turn out not to be. For instance, England's home draw against Macedonia was thought to make direct qualification for England very difficult indeed; but although losing that game may have dented confidence, when looking at the final table, England could have afforded to have lost (even heavily) and still to have won the group. Here then is the story of all the ups and downs on the way to Portugal 2004, including what turned out to be crucial in terms of how the teams that got there, got there!

GROUP I:
Could They Make it Any Easier for France?

No, not really. Whilst it has to be said that in recent years Cyprus have managed to put together the odd decent result (including a surprise 3-2 victory against Spain) and whilst Slovenia emerged as a pretty decent football team, this was never really going to test the French, notwithstanding their goal-shy World Cup and the fact that Israel had interfered with their plans in the past, not least in terms of the 1994 World Cup when the Bulgarians applied the coup de grace in Paris.[1]

But I digress. Actually, while I digress, I shall digress further. How do Israel get in Europe? Of course the answer is that the other children in their own playground won't play nicely with them so they come and play in Europe. Ooh I could go off on one about Israel. A state based on (i.e. founded by) terrorism which now slaughters the people who had been living in Palestine for thousands of years, and all – apparently – as part of a war against terrorism. What's that all about? How can a people who suffered so terribly inflict such suffering on others? And why does no one seem to understand that fighting terror with terror will always simply engender more terror. It's shocking. [Editor's note: The subsequent 8,000-word tirade by Dr Pettiford, railing against the global injustices of Bush's 'new world order' and Israel's place in it has had to

[1] Kostadinov in the last minute I think, but I never can remember!

be deleted. If you do happen to be interested in such observations, we can do no better than direct you to another Arcturus publication *Terrorism: The New World War,* (2003) by, er, Lloyd Pettiford and David Harding].

Apologies for the bit of politics. Anyway, this group never looked likely to test the French – that's the point – and with one non-European without a history of major competition success (Israel) and two islands (Cyprus and Malta) for competition, it was perhaps the most predictable of groups in terms of the runners-up spot too, which Slovenia took with some ease, building on their remarkable progress over a few short years. In 1998 World Cup qualifying the Slovenians had managed just one point from eight games, and yet in qualifying for Japan/Korea they went 12 games undefeated; winning five and drawing five in qualifying was enough to earn a play-off spot where they surprised many by beating Romania at home and drawing away to get through.

Looking at qualifying for this group it is difficult to find a surprise of any kind. France won all their games. Slovenia lost to France and were held to a draw in Israel but otherwise cruised into the play-off spot without ever looking – from the moment of their 5-0 defeat in France in October 2003 – like challenging for direct qualification. In fact what with having qualified as holders for the World Cup in 2002 (did I mention the fact that they failed to score so much as a goal in their defence of the title?) you could almost say it is a long long time since France had a genuinely competitive game!

The biggest win in the group was France's 6-0 demolition of Malta, with 6 also being the highest game aggregate (in that game). The biggest away win was Malta 0-4 France. Unsurprisingly Malta finished bottom of the group, surprisingly earning their only point in a 2-2 draw away to Israel.

Quick Quiz

1. In the year before the end of the qualifying tournament how many teams did France not beat?

2. Which tournament did France win in 2003?

3. Why was France's 1-0 win against Cameroon especially hollow?

4. At the time of writing (October 2003) who were the last team not to lose to France apart from the Czech Republic?

5. If France were so stunning in 2002/03 how come they were so, frankly, pathetic in defence of their world crown in 2002?

6. What was the difference in attendance between the final qualifying games on 11 October 2003?

Answers

1: One. They lost to the Czech Republic 2-0 but won 15 other games   2: The Confederations Cup   3: The win, in the final of The Confederations Cup, came after Marc-Vivien Foe of the Cameroon had collapsed and died in the semi-final   4: Tunisia, who earned a 1-1 home draw in a friendly in August 2002   5: Who cares. Quite funny though   6: A lot. Cyprus v Slovenia attracting less than 2,500 and France v Israel over 57,000

GROUP 2:
The Luck of the Scandinavians

If Group 1 was Dullsville City, Arizona[2] then Group 2 was
surprisingly close – and filled with surprises – with
Denmark qualifying direct and the Norwegians somehow
making the play-offs at the expense of the Romanians,
Bosnians and Herzegovians (the last two playing as one).
Romania, being the team who would sit out the final round
of matches, needed to win in Denmark to guarantee a play-
off spot and give themselves a genuine shot at automatic
qualification. Deep into injury time they led 2-1. At about
the same time Bosnia-Herzegovina were clinging
tenaciously to a 1-0 lead in Luxembourg. Combined with
their home win against Luxembourg, a 1-0 win against
Norway in the previous game and a surprise 2-0 win in
Denmark, that gave them a shot at – amazingly – winning
the group if they could win their last game – at home to the
very same Denmark.

Speak to your average Romanian on the subject of that
last game of theirs and one gets the impression that the
similarities between the Danish and Swiss flags is enough
to explain their elimination from Portugal 2004, the referee
of that fateful game in Copenhagen being a certain Herr
Maier from Switzerland. He had already awarded the Danes
a penalty from which they took the lead in the first half,
only to be pegged back by Mutu and Pancu in the second
half. It is one of those games where the 'raw' statistic

[2] Copyright: That character in *The Fall and Rise of Reginald Perrin*.

'Laursen 90' hides so much. Herr Maier having signalled (a minimum of) four minutes of added time 'allowed' the Danes to equalise in the fifth minute. (Besides that game, the Romanians must be kicking themselves for allowing late goals to drop points both at home and away to Norway, and for collapsing when in control at home to Denmark).

Personally, I have little sympathy with the Romanians. For a start the whole 'added time' thing comes with a warning as clear as the ones about investments going up as well as down and about your house being taken away if you don't keep up repayments on a loan. There will be a minimum of so many minutes added time. Furthermore, if you want my opinion the Romanians are a bunch of cheating diving b****** who were probably wasting so much time in the last few minutes that Herr Maier was fully justified in adding on the extra time. Although not based on actually having seen the match, this opinion is strictly impartial and based on the finest traditions of journalistic integrity. I am not swayed at all by having stood on an open terrace getting rained on heavily for three hours whilst watching the Romanian national tumbling team (aka Steaua Bucharest) dive and connive their way to a thoroughly unjust UEFA cup victory against the forces of truth and goodness embodied by Southampton FC. By the way, 'Steaua' rhymes with 'dour'. [Editor's note: Again we have been forced to remove another extensive tirade, entitled 'Why Does It Always Rain on Me?', this time against Romanian taxi drivers (b******) and the inadequacy of toilet facilities at Steaua Stadium].

So, the Danes' draw at home to Romania meant that

they needed another away to Bosnia-Herzegovina to win the group, whilst the poor old Romanians were relying on Luxembourg (goals for: none, goals against: 20 in the first seven qualifiers) to nick a point in Norway if they were to have any chance. Their only hope perhaps lay in the fact that Norway – the team that was recently beating Brazil in the World Cup – were now absolutely sh*t and almost as shot-shy as the Greeks. [Editor's Note: See elsewhere for indignant tirade against Greek 'strikers'].

In the event it all still went to the wire. Denmark got the draw they needed in Bosnia, but no more than that. A goal for Bosnia would have seem them pip Denmark by a point leaving Denmark, Norway and Romania level on points. The Romanians still wouldn't have qualified, not in a month of injury time. But Bosnia did not get the goal in any case. Meanwhile, Norway, won 1-0 at home to Luxembourg. This put them level on points with Romania and gave them a goal-difference of +4 compared to the Romanians +12. However, the 1-0 win for Norway in Bucharest (83 minutes, bloody hell Stefan Iversen scored a goal!) coupled with a late equalising penalty in Oslo (Solskjaer, poor old Romanians) allowed the desperate Norwegians to scrape into the play-offs (of which more below).

The highest home win in the group was Romania's 4-0 win against Luxembourg. Romania's 7-0 win in Luxembourg was the highest away win. Seven goals was the joint highest aggregate for a match, with Luxembourg v Romania equalled by Romania 2-5 Denmark, a game in which Denmark trailed 2-1 with around 35 minutes to go!

Quick Quiz

1. True or false? Romania, who failed to qualify, scored more goals than both group winners Denmark and runners-up Norway.

2. Bottom team Luxembourg were one of three teams to not score in eight games. Who were the others?

3. True or false? Of the teams not scoring Luxembourg conceded fewest goals?

4. Which British-based player scored Norway's goal in their crucial 1-0 win versus Luxembourg?

5. In Norway's game against Luxembourg, who was the only member of the back four not based in England?

6. In January 2003 how many turned up to watch Oman versus Norway in a friendly?

Answers

1: True. Romania's 21 topped Denmark's 15 and Norway's 9 and was almost as much as the two combined! 2: San Marino and Northern Ireland 3: False. Northern Ireland conceded only eight goals in fact 4: Tore Andre Flo 5: Basma of Rosenberg, who was joined by Santa Claus Lundekvam of the Super Saints, Henning Berg and John Arne Riise 6: A somewhat disappointing 500

GROUP 3:
Will Austria Ever Again Have a Football Team?

In some ways, the excitement never started in Group 3. The Czechs were a bit better than the Dutch. The Dutch were better than the Austrians, who were better than the Moldovans who outshone the Belarussians. In the end, the Czechs' 3-1 home win against Holland in September 2003 in Prague, enjoyed by fewer than go to Hull City home games, turned out to be the group decider, condemning *la naranja mecanica* (Spanish for 'bunch of in-fighting posers') of Holland to the play-offs where they didn't – *quelle surprise* (that's French for 'it's a fix') – get Turkey or Spain.

In fact the group might have been a good deal closer in normal circumstances but the Czechs performed beyond theirs and anybody else's expectations. After disappointing in the World Cup qualifiers for 2002, and trailing 1-0 at half time in Rotterdam, few would have predicted how easily they would control the group once the huge ungainly Koller had equalised in that match. True, even then the home win against Holland was eventually the only difference between the sides, but after an away win versus France in a friendly, the Czechs' confidence was sky high. They won the match against Holland 3-1, with Milan Baros settling nerves with a last-minute goal after the Czechs had led comfortably at the break.

Both Holland and the Czech Republic recorded 5-0 home wins over Moldova and Austria produced the same

score against Belarus, whilst the highest away win was
Holland's in Austria early in the campaign (3-0). The
highest aggregate in a game was five, in the home victories
noted above and also in the Czechs' 3-2 win in Vienna.

Quick Quiz

1 Wouldn't it have been simpler just to let the Czechs and Dutch play each other to see who qualified?

2 Against whom did Belarus' single win come?

3 Where did Belarus score their single away goal?

4 In this context, why was the only other goal managed by the Belarussians special?

5 Can't you think of any questions more interesting than this?

6 In the Czech's final game, Koller's last-minute goal gave them a 3-2 win. What was the score when Austria's Schopp was sent off in the 63rd minute and why did this matter?

Answers

1: Yes, although the Czech coach was very keen to repeat the mantra about no easy games in international football after the opening game win in Moldova **2:** Moldova 2-1 on 29 March 2003 **3:** Surprising no one I'm sure – Moldova **4:** It came at home to the group-winning Czechs and took the lead in the 14th minute. A lead they held for over 20 minutes. Only a goal in the last five minutes from Vlad the Incapable – I mean Smicer – settled Czech nerves in a 3-1 win **5:** No, it was a rather boring group **6:** 1-0 to Austria and it didn't matter at all

GROUP 4:

Oh Puskas, Wherefore Art Thou?

With the Latvian 'Michael Owen' aka the 'Little Latvian' or 'Super Marian' Pahars injured for most of the qualifying matches, Latvia had to go through Euro-qualifying with a collection of players of a roughly equivalent standard to – no offence – Grimsby Reserves. What a pleasant surprise it must have been then to pip a Polish side who qualified easily for the 2002 World Cup and a Hungarian side with a great footballing tradition to a play-off place. For the rest of us, it was probably the surprise of the qualifyiers, with Latvia languishing at around 70 in FIFA rankings. However, with the final group matches pairing Hungary and Poland and leaving Latvia to travel to group leaders and winners Sweden, things went right to a rather nervous wire for the middle one of the Baltic Republics.

Poland must really be wondering about the Swedes! The group looked to be between them and the Swedes but after the first few matches they were already playing catch up with a Latvian team that went to Warsaw and won 1-0. True the Poles subsequently won 2-0 in Riga but the slow-starting – then group-winning Swedes – had the 'casting vote'. Back in 1999 it was the Swedes who won what for them was a dead match against Poland, which meant that England qualified for the play-offs (which they won against Scotland). This time around, Poland might have expected that their last-day win in Hungary would put them level on points with Latvia and with a 2-1 aggregate win in head to head matches. But no, Latvia actually won in Sweden.

Ultimately, Latvia took four points off Sweden whilst Poland got none (as was the case in 2000 qualifying).

San Marino was one of the teams which failed to score, and of those the one which conceded most goals. The highest home win in the group was 5-0 which both Poland and Sweden managed against the tiny Italian thing. The biggest away win was 6-0 by Sweden in San Marino, with six also being the highest aggregate score for a game. San Marino's best result was a 1-0 home defeat to the little Latvians, who many will feel were very lucky to have made the play-offs, although then again any team that beats Sweden must be pretty good; England never do it!

Quick Quiz

1. True or false? Southampton would probably have beaten boring boring Arsenal in the 2003 FA Cup and even more dour Steaua Bucharest in the 2003 UEFA Cup if Marian Pahars had been fit.

2. Why were Latvia hanging on in their final group game away in Sweden?

3. Apart from group winners Sweden (+16), who had the best goal difference in the group?

4. Apart from the free-missing San Marino team which team in the group found the net fewest times?

5. Did Latvia get the round thing in the net more often at home or away?

6. Latvia got the most successful tournament in their history off to a great start by drawing 0-0 at home to Sweden. Only 8,500 saw the game. But by how much had crowds swelled by the time of their last home qualifier, a 3-1 and decisive thumping of the Hungarians?

Answers

1: Almost certainly true according to any Saints fan 2: Not only were they facing the combined might of Michael and Anders Svensson, but also reduced to 10 men in the 73rd minute 3: Fourth placed Hungary with +6 4: Latvia 5: At home, thanks to getting three against both Hungary and San Marino 6: The crowd had, in fact, dwindled to 7,500

47

GROUP 5:
The League of Super Minnows

First they organise a special Korean World Cup to ensure
Germany qualify for the final and then they manage to
arrange a European qualifying group of various pathetic
minnow nations so that qualifying isn't too onerous a task.
Rumour has it that the German psyche was so profoundly
affected by the 5-1 rout by England that several billion euros
changed hands to ensure that if Germany were to draw a
home nation it would be a nice easy one like Scotland. As an
added precaution the Germans decided to manage the
Scottish team too. There is, of course, absolutely no
substance in *any* of the above, which represents nothing
more than a gratuitous excuse to mention beating Germany
5-1 combined with unnecessary Anglo arrogance/anti-
Scottishness. I should apologise for this, but decline to.
[Editor's note: We should really delete this kind of jibbering
jingoistic nonsense, but if you take out his anti-Israeli stuff
and tirades against Bucharest taxi drivers too, it gets pretty
hard to pad this thing out. Besides, he's cheap and no one
else offered to churn out 60,000 words in a fortnight. I
mean, how much did you pay for this? It's a bargain really].

Theoretically, Iceland could have condemned Germany
to a play-off spot by winning their final game in Germany.
But that was never going to happen was it? Even so, the
Germans made *hugely* heavy weather of things up to that
point. At home they defeated the Faroes 2-1 with the aid of
a penalty. Away in the Faroes they didn't score until the
89th minute before winning 2-0. They also drew at home

to Lithuania and away to Scotland and Iceland. But even so, by the time the group was over, they had won five games and drawn three to qualify both undefeated and unimpressive.

Of those chasing second spot, the Lithuanians impressed except against Iceland to whom they managed to lose 3-0, twice. This left the way open for either Iceland, if they won in Germany or Scotland failed to beat Lithuania, or to Scotland, if they beat Lithuania. And, Lithuania being less formidable than the likes of Costa Rica, Iran or Peru (again, unnecessary and gratuitous) the Scots romped home 1-0 with a late goal and qualified for a play-off against the only team they ever got a decent result against, Holland. (For my predictable play-off predictions and whether they came true, see below!)

A statistic the Faroes would probably have settled for before qualifying is that the biggest win in the group – home or away – was 3-0 and neither included the Faroes ('We're hard to beat' claims manager Henrik Larson – no, not that one). This was achieved at home by Germany against Iceland, and Iceland against Lithuania and away by Iceland against Lithuania. The highest aggregate score was a mere four goals, this number being racked up in three games; Faroes draw against Scotland and two 3-1 victories against the Faroes (Scotland v Faroes and Faroes v Lithuania).

Quick Quiz

(1) Despite a goal difference of only –11 in eight games, the Faroe Islands only managed to pick up a single point in qualifying. Against which team?

(2) Given that San Marino, Northern Ireland and Luxembourg failed to find the net at all in qualifying, what Impressive percentage of games did the Faroes find the net in?

(3) Isn't that better than Scotland?

(4) OK then, but it must be better than the others in the group?

(5) Of the final group games, which drew the bigger crowd: Germany v Iceland or Scotland v Lithuania?

(6) Berti Vogts?

Answers

1: Scotland   2: 75%   3: No, the Scots only failed to score in losing 1-0 in Lithuania
4: Yes. Apart from Germany who only failed to score in a 0-0 draw away to Iceland, Iceland failed to score on three occasions and Lithuania four compared to the Faroes two
5: By 50,780 to 50,343 slightly more people were in Hamburg than Glasgow   6: No

GROUP 6:
It's a Funny Old Game

Spain (with Raul etc etc etc), Ukraine (Shevchenko etc), Greece (the bloke that looks like George Clooney in goal), Armenia, Northern Ireland. Pick two to qualify. Simple eh? Spain to win the group and Ukraine to go into a play-off. Amongst the first two sets of matches, now add the following results. Greece 0-2 Spain. Ukraine 2-0 Greece. At this point you're prepared to put your house on either Spain or Ukraine to win the group and uninterested in betting so much as sixpence on Greece to win the group, or anything else, for that matter. But incredibly that's what happened, as George Cloonyadis and the boys won six consecutive matches without conceding a goal.

True the '1-0 with a penalty' win against Northern Ireland which clinched top spot doesn't fill fellow qualifiers with dread, but the crucial 1-0 home win against Ukraine (Haristeas getting the winner in the last five minutes) was impressive, even if only 15,000 were there to be impressed. But perhaps most extraordinarily, just four days before that win, Greece had travelled to Zaragoza and sneaked another 1-0, stubbornly defending for the second half after Giannakopoulos (that's Bolton's Stelios to you and me) had given them the lead on the stroke of half time. David Coleman would say 'Er, quite extraordinary' and Dangermouse would say 'Good grief Penfold'. And you know what? They're both right.

At the other end of the table, and keeping up with the Luxembourgeois, Northern Ireland failed to score a goal.

Twenty years after beating the host nation Spain in the World Cup – and notwithstanding a solid 0-0 at home to them this time which gave the group to Greece – it's been a steep decline for the team so proudly represented by stars such as George Best, Gerry Armstrong, Norman Whiteside and Iain Dowie [Iain, if you ever read this, that sentence surely merits a £500 donation to Shelter. I mean I know you and George have a lot in common but...]. Anyhoo, rumours that the country is to change its name to 'Northern Ireland Nil' have been slightly exaggerated – but only slightly.[3]

After their 0-0 draw in Belfast, Spain had to rely on Greece slipping up. Although this might have been expected, it didn't happen and Spain would have to rely on the play-offs if they wanted to make the short Iberian journey to the 2004 finals. The Ukraine, losing only twice and narrowly (away to Spain and Greece) paid the price of too many draws, surrendering a 2-0 lead away to Armenia going into the last 20 minutes, a 1-0 lead going into the last 10 minutes against Spain and, probably most disappointingly, only drawing at home against Northern Ireland Nil. Apart from their point against Ukraine, Armenia – along with Greece – did the double over the Irish, er British, er Northern Irish. [Editor's Note: Another 30-page essay on the complexities of Irish history since 1344 was deleted here].

And so Greece headed for Portugal, Spain to the play-offs, Armenia to the Black Sea (probably) and Northern Ireland back to the drawing board, hopefully with a big picture of a posty/cross-bar-ry/netty thing on it. It truly is a

[3] And it seems almost inevitable that their first competitive goal in a long time will come against England in the World Cup...

funny old game. Biggest home win in the group came as Spain beat both Northern Ireland and Armenia 3-0 and the biggest away win was Spain's 4-0 victory in Armenia. Highest aggregate was the match between Ukraine and Armenia. Armenia took a shook lead but went in at half time at 1-1. After half time they quickly regained the lead again only for Shevchenko to bang in a couple. Although the Armenians equalised almost immediately, Fedorov popped up in the last minute to give Ukraine a 4-3 victory. The kind of game the Greeks don't get involved in.

Quick Quiz

1. Northern Ireland conceded eight goals in qualifying. 60% of all teams and 100% of teams in Group 10 conceded more. True or false?

2. Apart from France, did anyone in qualifying win more consecutive games than Greece?

3. True or false? All the group's 0-0 draws involved Northern Ireland Nil.

4. Who was the only team in the group to score more goals than it got points?

5. Which of Greece's players plays for the famous Aigaleo team?

6. That last question suggests I'm scraping around a bit for ideas and should probably take a rest?

Answers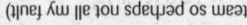

1: True   2: No. England and the Czech Republic both managed five consecutively but Greece won their last six qualifiers   3: True. Three of them   4: Ukraine whose 11 goals earned only 10 points   5: Er, Anastasios Agritis whose one cap at the time of writing came against Cyprus in a friendly in front of 2000 people   6: Yes, but Greece really are a dull team so perhaps not all my fault!

GROUP 7:
You're Gonna Get Your F****** 'eads Kicked In

Well if this wasn't quite back to the 'Match of the 70s' in terms of hooliganism, it did seem – lovely Liechtenstein excepted – that this was the group of racist and/or violent fans. In this context, it is difficult to fathom how a small celebratory pitch invasion seems to be regarded as worse by UEFA than hurling bottles onto the pitch or incessant taunting of black English players. National anthem booing is not in the same league. Clearly, England still have a hooligan problem, and with things under control at home it has to a certain extent been displaced abroad, where the lager is stronger and the licensing laws less ridiculous. But to some extent it is an issue of reputation. Ask anyone who has been to a match in Italy recently whether England has a hooligan problem! And in the UEFA Cup and Champions League Blackburn can travel to Turkey without problem, whilst a legion of riot police stood looking absolutely bewildered at the 2,500 smiling Southampton fans who reacted to defeat by Steaua with an intimidating round of applause for the home team.

As for the group itself, it looked like it was all going to go horribly wrong at one point, but Sven's men – with the exception of one game against the world champions – always look capable of retrieving a situation. In both qualifiers against Slovakia they trailed 1-0 at half-time but won 2-1. At home to Macedonia they were losing twice in Southampton but salvaged a point; at the time this was regarded by some as a disaster but was ultimately enough. Away to Macedonia England also trailed at half time. Even Liechtenstein held England to 0-0 at half-time in England and restricted England to four goals in two matches. In fact England's ability to get the right result, and if not the best result, at least a result, from matches in which they struggled and trailed is quite remarkable.

Oddly, it is against Turkey that England seemed to have fewest problems. Despite not scoring until late, England's 2-0 win at home was a performance of pace and power, in stark contrast to the previous game in Liechtenstein. Away from home against the Turks, and without fans, England's performance was even more remarkable. England dominated. After David Beckham had taken his Jonny Wilkinson impression a step too far, hoofing the ball 40 yards over the bar from a penalty, and Scholes had missed an eminently presentable chance, it seemed England may have made the mistake of failing to score whilst on top. But as you might have expected the jitters to strike, and needing only a point, England remained steadfast and were able to celebrate alone in the stadium, joined by millions at home. The unbiased and hugely authoritative presence of referee Pierluigi Collina ensured that the 'crowd effect' was minimised in terms of outrageous home decisions.

With England and Turkey out front and them playing last, despite Sven's comeback kings keeping the nation on its toes, it always seemed that the real interest in the group would boil down to that one match. So it proved. One of the more amusing moments therefore from the many group games surrounded the playing of the national anthems against Liechtenstein, with both teams using the same 'tune'. Apparently this was rather less amusing when Eire had visited Liechtenstein as many in the crowd assumed that some terrible faux pas had been made. So, England avoided a play-off against the mighty Latvians. The final league table includes little of interest, including the fact that Macedonia's record of five more goals than points is one of the highest in qualifying – equalled by France and bettered only by the Faroes (six) and poor old tumbling Romania (seven).

The highest home win in the group was Turkey's 5-0 win against Liechtenstein. The highest away win came in the return fixture with the Turks winning 3-0. The highest aggregate score for a game was five: the one referred to above, plus Turkey's exciting 3-2 home win against Macedonia in which the Macedonians led twice and at half time as against England.

Quick Quiz

(1) Which team in the group had the biggest d***head supporters?

(2) In total, how many times did the Macedonian team manage to take the lead against England and Turkey?

(3) How many points did Macedonia secure from its four games against the group's top two teams?

(4) Which game drew the bigger crowd, Liechtenstein v Turkey or Liechtenstein v England?

(5) Do people ever make up statistics like crowds?

(6) Stengthening the argument for greater Asian representation at the World Cup (not) which game did Liechtenstein manage to win in 2003 against a team represented in Japan/South Korea 2002 and how many people showed up to watch?

Answers

1: This is difficult to say, but we should remember that England is easily 'up there' in any d***head table and beware of turning the whole argument into a rather essentialising, casual anti-Turk racism. Some of my best friends are Turkish. That said, what they have done to their Kurdish minority is disgraceful...[Editor's Notes: Despite the systematic murder and torture in 'Turkish' Kurdistan and the numerous judgements against the Turkish state on human rights issues by – for instance – the European Court of Human Rights, I'm afraid we had to cut him off again then. I mean he just goes on and on. This is a football book f'crissakes.] 2: Six 3: Just the one, at the St Mary's stadium, home of Southampton FC 4: According to the well known magazine World Soccer, both matches attracted 3,548 supporters. Maybe that's the capacity or someone just got lazy? 5: 76.89% of people do, yes 6: Liechtenstein beat Saudi Arabia 1-0 on 30 April 2003 with 1,200 in attendance

GROUP 8:
Thank Goodness For The Beer

Talking of casual racism and stereotyping – as I was in the last section – Belgium often gets a raw deal. But far from being boring – as it is sometimes unfairly cast – it is absolutely fascinating as Harry Pearson's book *Tall Man in a Low Land* makes clear. Personally, I can never be bored as long as someone is prepared to put a steak in green pepper-cream sauce with chips and beer in front of me, but as well as that many Belgian towns are rather quaint and the beer comes in so many different types and flavours it is bewildering. Even more bewildering is the fact that so many English visitors do little more than quaff too much Stella and say 'yuk, this beer's cloudy' or words to that effect when given something else. So take your holidays in Belgium. It's often weird but – if they had a hillside – it'd be welcoming.

[Editor's note: Ahem...] Yes, OK, football...I was getting there. After losing their opening game at home to Bulgaria, then unimpressively sneaking wins (1-0 away) against Andorra and Estonia and losing 4-0 in Croatia, Belgium were always going to find things tough and indeed left themselves too much to do. Good job therefore that there's so much nice beer for them to drink as they miss out on Portugal 2004 (see it was relevant!). A better second half of the campaign saw them narrowly miss out on a play-off spot to Croatia who qualified ahead of Belgium thanks largely to that 4-0 victory and a better head-to-head record.

The Bulgarians romped home in the end, conceding few goals and only succumbing to defeat once qualification was already assured. Estonian football – unlike that of their Latvian neighbours – hasn't quite got going. Perhaps they had a few too many Sakus post-Communism (now Saku is nice beer!) but two wins against Andorra and a couple of 0-0 draws were their only reward this time around.

The group's biggest home win was Croatia's 4-0 victory against the *rode duivels/diables rouges* of Belgium. Both Bulgaria and Croatia won 3-0 in Andorra and no one managed to beat four goals in a game, with Bulgaria and Belgium equalling that total set by Croatia-Belgium, but on this occasion in a 2-2 draw.

Quick Quiz

(1) Group 8 was the lowest scoring group. True or false?

(2) Which group competed with Group 8 as the lowest scoring one?

(3) Are Bulgarians interested in friendlies?

(4) In what percentage of Group 8 matches did both teams score?

(5) Did Group 8 have the most 0-0 draws?

(6) Where did Andorra score their only qualifying goal?

Answers

1: True, with only 41 goals in 20 matches   2: Group 6, which managed 42 despite the group winners managing just eight and Northern Ireland getting none   3: No. Whilst 40,000+ turned up for their European qualifiers, including against Andorra, a friendly against Germany attracted just 10,000   4: Only 15%   5: No, that was Group 6, where the Northern Irish were involved in them all   6: In Sofia against group winners Bulgaria, producing a nervy last 10 minutes for the home side, who held on to win 2-1

GROUP 9:
Oh Noah! It's Happened Again...

What a start for the Welsh. Winning away to Finland and at home to Italy. Add to that a couple of wins against Azerbaijan, and Wales was getting distinctly excited about sport for the first time since egg-chasers supreme Gareth Edwards, Phil Bennett, JPR Williams and Willie John McBride.[4] However, Wales were unable to pick up a single point against Serbia and Montenegro and could only draw at home to Finland, in the end rather fortunately. Their chance to qualify as group winners was slipping agonizingly away. But it was the game away to Italy which really ended Welsh hopes.

At least for the first half and a bit, one could only assume that either God was Welsh (which would have been a bit of a shock for Christianity which has, not unreasonably, always assumed him to be English) or that Paul Jones had erected some kind of force-field around his goal. Whichever explanation one chooses to accept, it all went horribly wrong in 10 second-half minutes when Filippo Inzaghi knocked in a hat-trick. Either God had nipped out to tend his leaks and daffs, or a power surge in the Romulan sector had seen force-fields affected across the galaxy. Either way, Del Piero added a penalty and one could sense further tears and play-off heartbreak for the Welsh.

[4] Willie John was of course Irish, but people always like to look at books and point out the errors.

The footballers formally known as Yugoslavia must have been gutted, sick as a parrot etc. They drew twice against group winners Italy and beat play-off qualifiers Wales twice and yet still failed to progress! Amazingly, this is because in a show of 'we were all communists once' solidarity, they provided table-proppers Azerbaijan with all of their four points (as well as losing in Finland). Not only that, but at home Serbia and Montenegro were 2-0 up (drawing 2-2) and away they were winning 1-0 with five minutes to go and conceded two goals in five minutes. I mean Azerbaijan only scored one other goal (than their four v Serbia and Montenegro) in the whole qualifying campaign and that was in a 2-1 defeat at home to Finland! So you can go on all you like about a renaissance in Welsh football but really the former Yugoslavs just threw it away big time and should really have been in those play-offs.

As if to emphasise the above, the group's biggest home wins were Italy's and Wales' 4-0 victories over Azerbaijan together with Italy's 4-0 win against Wales. Away performances were less impressive with the biggest margin being 2-0 on four separate occasions. The highest aggregate score for a match was five when Serbia and Montenegro won in Cardiff 3-2 – not that it mattered of course.

Quick Quiz

1. Which Group 9 team changed its name during qualifying?

2. Apart from Azerbaijan (twice) where did Finland's other win come?

3. What was the most impressive statistic about Wales' qualifying campaign in relation to the same statistic of any other team?

4. What, even better than Italy's, Germany's etc?

5. Do Azerbaijan ever beat anybody? (I mean notwithstanding buggering up Serbia and Montenegro's chances)

6. Wales managed it a few times, but when was the last time Scotland scored against the Finns?

Answers

1: Serbia and Montenegro, who had previously been Yugoslavia   2: 3-0 at home to Serbia and Montenegro   3: Their crowds, regularly weighing in at 72,000 plus   4: Yes, Italy's biggest crowd was the 68,000 who turned up to see Wales. As for Germans and the rest, good but not that good!   5: Yes, Uzbekistan were soundly thrashed 2-0 in Baku in August 2002 for instance, but they did provide a rare moment of sporting success for Liechtenstein, who beat them 2-1 in 1997   6: For those racking their brains for the last Finland v Scotland fixture, the rather disappointing news is that the answer is 29 January 2003 when a player called Scotland scored for Trinidad and Tobago in a friendly which the Finns won 2-1

GROUP 10:
Who Are Ya?

Much wailing and gnashing of teeth was effected by
football pundits in the UK, who seem to have rather fallen
into the trap of assuming the Republic of Ireland – or Eire –
to be one of the home nations. The former management by
Jack Charlton and the array of cockney accents in the team
might have led you to this conclusion. However, in
appointing an Irish manager or two and in toning down
their success levels, Eire are doing their best to prove
they're not England in disguise. (Ooh that sounds far too
arrogant even for the tongue in cheek jingoism so far –
sincere apologies, especially to Orla Benson, Allen White
and that bloke I met in a pub in Liverpool when Saints drew
0-0 and 'if Heskey plays for England so can I'...)

This wasn't going to be their (Eire's) qualifying
tournament. Although Greece proved what might be
achieved after a poor start, the away loss to Russia and
home defeat by Switzerland in the first two games always
suggested that these teams would head the group instead
of the Irish. Despite recovering to give themselves a
chance by the final game, it was one they were unable to
take, losing in Switzerland who won the group. Russia, like
Southampton in 2003 he mentioned gratuitously, headed
for the Millennium Stadium, Cardiff.

At the other end of the table Georgia struggled, but must
have taken great pleasure in a 1-0 home win against Russia.
Similarly Albania. A win in either game – or indeed a draw
– would have given Russia the group and condemned

Switzerland to the play-offs. Lots of strange results between these former communists you notice.

The biggest home wins came for Russia, who beat group winners Switzerland and Georgia 4-1. Away results were less impressive with only two away wins of any kind. Switzerland's win in Dublin was crucial (2-1) and equalled in scoring terms the Irish's own win in Georgia (which was less so). The highest aggregate for a game was six in the opening match between Russia and the Irish Republic, which the home team won 4-2.

Quick Quiz:

Special Focus on Georgia

Apart from Stalin and having the same name as a US state, Georgia has failed to grab enough attention in the past. We rectify that here with a very special feature which emerges, quite simply, as a result of getting bored with these quizzes.

1 Dinamo Batumi is a football team in Georgia. True or false?

2 What about Torpedo Kutaisi, WIT Georgia and Zalaegerszeg then?

3 Is Temuri Ketsbaia, formerly of Newcastle, the most capped of current Georgian players?

4 Has Georgi Kinkladze scored more goals for Georgia than any other player in the current Georgian squad?

5 Who's the oldest player Georgia currently field?

6 What was Georgia's best win in the year after the World Cup?

Answers

6: Their only win, but what a win, against the Russians

assuming you read this in 2004 after March and they are still picking him

20 first. Kinky's not yet reached 10 for all his trickery   5: Temuri again, who's now 36 –

Arveladze and the afore mentioned Temuri Ketsbaia are battling it out to see who can get to

Hungarian   3: No, some chap called Georgi Nemsadze has more   4: Oh no, Shota

1: Oh yes, very true   2: Again yes, they're all teams, although the latter is quite clearly

The Play-Offs

The satisfaction of playing appallingly and only winning one match except for Luxembourg, then relying on Sweden beating Poland (twice) and then losing 1-0 to Scotland and *still* qualifying for Euro 2000 cannot be denied. However, it was nice to avoid all that this time and watch the agonies of others from afar, not least because this allowed the author the luxury of a whole extra month to write this book, which was only ever going to be commissioned once England had qualified. Such are the harsh realities of the capitalist world that it was felt that you – the great 'British' public – would only buy this book in sufficient quantities if Eng-er-land had already qualified. Too right! So to the play-offs of which there were five for the remaining five places after an agonising wait (ha! ha!) of over a month for the fans of the countries involved.

Since this book was prepared ready for publication prior to Christmas 2003, as I write, the clocks have just gone back and it is 27 October 2003. Since all the following ties were played between the 15 and 19 November I take the opportunity to predict the outcomes of the play-offs. You have only my word, of course, that I did not tinker with these results, but I hope that is enough for you.[5] My word is my bond. So, below, I suspect I will either be crowing about my fantastic predictions or feverishly explaining away their inaccuracy. This is the man who predicted Senegal as the shock of World Cup 2002, but this should give you an idea of how seriously to take my predictions later on in the book.

[5] The fact I got them all wrong might also convince you!

Croatia v Slovenia: Winners Croatia

Prediction

The unpredictable Croats against the team that has become increasingly hard to beat. For Slovenia the unpredictable Zlatko Zahovic may well be the key. Imagine having the initials ZZ and still being only the second best player in the world to have them!

Prediction: Croatia 2-1 Slovenia and Slovenia 2-0 Croatia (in my extremely humble opinion, the most likely tie to result in a shock)

What really happened – first leg

Croatia 1–1 Slovenia (November 15)

Well, not spot on, but Croatia very much in the driving seat. Only the most extraordinary tip onto the post from goal scorer Dado Prso prevented the predicted result.

What really happened – second leg

Slovenia 0–1 Croatia (November 19)

Predicted as the one shock, ultimately I'm glad that the one shock wasn't this. Having negotiated play-offs in the last two tournaments, however, Slovenia must have thought they were going to do it. With the crucial away goal and still drawing 0-0 at home, Croatia had Tudor sent off after 58 minutes leaving the Slovenians a little over half an hour to hold out. As it happens Prso scored for Croatia almost immediately. This left the Slovenians half an hour to save the game, which they failed to do and never looked like doing. Prediction very wrong, but this was always going to be tight.

Latvia v Turkey: Winners Latvia

Prediction

The best version of this story would involve Marian Pahars knocking in a couple of hat-tricks for Southampton before knocking in a third in three games for the Latvians. However the Latvians are probably wondering how they got this far and Southampton fans are wondering if they will ever see the great – though little – Latvian again. Won't be plain sailing for the Turks but almost.

Prediction: Latvia 0-1 Turkey and Turkey 2-0 Latvia

What really happened – first leg

Latvia 1–0 Turkey (November 15)

Well you never know, I might ultimately be right about Turkey qualifying, but far from plain sailing! Verpakovskis – who scored the winner – had already had an effort cleared off the line before his cool finish in the 29th minute. Turkey had a player sent off and in total have three now ineligible for the second leg.

What really happened – second leg

Turkey 2–2 Latvia (November 19)

Now this was the shock. Not predicted by me but welcome all the same! I have changed my best version to mean Pahars recovering fitness to partner Verpakovskis next summer, having led Southampton back to the Millennium Stadium and victory this time. But you know what I'm like with predictions! But beyond Latvia qualifying perhaps the biggest shock was the manner in which they did it. Leading 2-0 with 25 minutes to go, many would have assumed that Turkey would either play out time, or get the third which would have made them safe. However, it was not to be.

One of Turkey's suspendees was the goalkeeper Rustu. His replacement fumbled a free-kick into his own net on 66 minutes. Even now one might have backed Turkey to go on and secure victory with a third. But no, that man Verpakovskis – the new Marian Pahars? – outpaced the Turkish defence to equalise on the night. Turkey now needed two goals to qualify and never looked like getting them. Can you imagine if England had lost in Turkey and then lost a play-off to Latvia having led with 25 minutes to go at home? No, neither can I! Maybe the fact that Latvia went into these play-offs unexpectedly after a morale-boosting win in Sweden and Turkey after the disappointment of again failing to score against England had something to do with it.

Russia v Wales. Winners Russia

Prediction

They really thought they'd do it this time, and much as I would be delighted if they did, I fear any Welshman reading this will be thinking 'if only'.

Prediction: Russia 2-0 Wales and Wales 1-1 Russia

What really happened - first leg

Russia 0-0 Wales (November 15)

Well it wasn't just me. Peter Jones (on Radio 5) said before the game that Wales would do well to hold it to 2-0 against a team which had notched an average of 3.75 goals a game at home in qualifying. But despite this excellent result, Wales are probably still underdogs.

What really happened - second leg

Wales 0-1 Russia (November 19)

It never really looked like it would happen for the Welsh and an early away goal dampened the spirits of the largest ever crowd for a football international at the Millennium Stadium at just over 73,000. When Wales needed luck they didn't get any. When they needed composure, they didn't get any. And when they needed to press forward and score, Russia just seemed to be controlling the game in cruise control. A shame, but in effect the games against Serbia and Montenegro were the crucial ones. Not the correct scores, but the correct team at least.

Scotland v Holland: Winners Holland

Prediction

How did it come to this? There used to be Dalglish and Law and Hansen. There used to be influential players with European Cup Winners medals without Scottish caps (John

McGovern) and now only players with FA Cup runners-up medals without Scottish caps (Paul Telfer). Alas, Scotland will be restricted to booing on England as usual, however much they lie back and think of Archie Gemmill.

Prediction: Scotland 1-2 Holland and Holland 1-1 Scotland

What really happened – first leg

Scotland 1–0 Holland (November 15)

Not as disastrously wrong a prediction as you would imagine! My 1-2 was predicated on an enterprising Scottish start. That they achieved. I then assumed the Dutch would storm back until the tie was safe and that Scotland might force a tense finish as the Dutch relaxed. All of this could still happen, although more of it might happen in Amsterdam than I had expected.

What really happened – second leg

Holland 6–0 Scotland (November 19)

No tense finish as Holland became the only play-off winners to play away first. Scotland failed to make this as close as I had suspected but surely no one actually expected them to do it? My prediction may have been wide of the mark (no one EVER predicts 6-0 unless they are eight years old or it's a game against San Marino) but I got the right team, and it was certainly much less silly than those who predicted Scottish glory and that Berti might actually be the right man for the job.

Spain v Norway: Winners Spain

Prediction

Sorry, Norwegians (not least cos they're all 6 foot 4 inches) but even including Latvia, Norway must be the poorest side in the play-offs. I could be wrong – and often am – but I predict an easy passage for Spain, before their usual pathetic capitulation in the finals!

Prediction: Spain 4-0 Norway and Norway 1-2 Spain

What really happened – first leg

Spain 2–1 Norway (November 15)

How is one to make reliable predictions if players like Stefan Iversen are going to score goals? Having given the Norwegians the lead, it then took Ruben Baraja's 85th minute effort to save the Spanish blushes, not to mention my own...I actually got one result (home win) correct, even if the score was hopelessly out. Spain, like Holland, Turkey and Russia, though must surely remain favourites? (My self respect is on the line!)

What really happened – second leg

Norway 0–3 Spain (November 19)

The Norwegian crowd must have been disappointed, but with the obvious exception of Claus Lundekvam (Norwegian Player of the Year 2003) the whole team has been disappointing. Playing against the highly ranked Spaniards victory was always unlikely even after taking the

lead in the first leg. The predicted aggregate of 6-1 turned out only to be 5-1 but the essential comfort of Spain's progress was even easier to predict than Holland's. The only people who must have been more disappointed than Norway were the Romanians, who would surely have been more of a match for Spain.

Conclusions

So, there you have it. In the end, shocks are few and far between. Most groups were won by the pre-tournament favourites (France, Denmark, Czech Republic, Sweden, Germany, England and Italy for instance) or where a favourite had been difficult to pick (Bulgaria and Switzerland). Where this conspicuously failed to happen – as in Group 6 – Spain then cruised through the play-offs. Holland also got through the play-offs, as did Russia. Having teams like Eire, Belgium, Romania and Scotland absent is not a huge surprise to anyone.

Finally, all the play-offs were won by the higher ranked team, except one. In that one, the 69th ranked Latvians came from behind to beat the team which finished third in the World Cup and which is ranked eighth in the FIFA world ranking. Yes, Latvia beat Turkey – the loveable team of Alpay, Sukur etc – and on what better note to finish this review?

Chapter 2

England's Qualifying Campaign – The Great Escape Part 2 (or 3)

Introduction

There is no doubt that England took huge strides under Sven Goran Eriksson. After Dietmar Hamann had depressingly scored the last ever goal at Wembley and Kevin Keegan admitted what the rest of us knew already, England's prospects of qualifying for Japan/Korea 2002 looked bleak. Howard Wilkinson's ability to get a 'nil' out of England as caretaker didn't help, although the 0-0 draw in Finland should have been a win – Ray Parlour's shot

clearly crossing the line, although being disallowed.

When Sven took over for that campaign people talked of England restructuring, playing younger players and forgetting even the possibility of making the next World Cup. That we did was a combination of excellent football and the fact that Sven, unlike Wilkinson in that away leg against Finland, looked like a lucky manager. England were going behind and winning and getting goals when they needed them. Most spectacularly in Germany, Sven and his team gave England a result so good that no one had even dreamed of it.

In the finals themselves, was the luck used up with Ronaldinho's freak free-kick over an uncertain Seaman? Whatever, England had a great tournament even if one couldn't help feeling that with France mis-firing appallingly, we really had missed a chance. However, after the position when Sven took over, a quarter-final loss to the winners and the knocking out of pre-tournament joint favourites Argentina was certainly a good result.

What it meant, of course, is that expectations – forever high with the English national team – had been raised even further. We had lost to the winners. Beaten one of the favourites. In first-halves at least played excellent football. The losing (thankfully) finalists Germany had been absolutely stuffed in qualifying 5-1. We now looked to have a group of players in their late 20s and sometimes early 30s who looked like Portugal 2004 would be the ideal time for them to win something.

In the way stood – it seemed – Turkey, who emerged during the World Cup to be rather stronger challengers than English people might have supposed. Turkey got third place and suffered only narrow defeats (at group and semi-stages) to Brazil. This was not the team England used to dispatch 8-0. So expectations were high, but qualification would not be easy; no-one wants to have to go through the play-offs and as Turkey who had to do that found out, anything can happen, including a side ranked 69 in the world beating a team that almost reached the World Cup final. Thankfully England sneaked it but it was story of twists, turns and drama. This match by match guide hopes to remind you of just some of it.

Slovakia 1 England 2 (Away – Bratislava)

With Sven's private life on the agenda more than football in the week leading up to the game, the England circus rolled into a very bleak Bratislava. It was raining and cold and a tricky first tie was assured. The pitch was as bumpy as the Slovak capital was bleak and England struggled to produce the football they know they can. Things looked ever bleaker (Sven must have wished he was home with Ulrika) when Middlesbrough's Nemeth gave the home side the lead. It was no more than the Slovaks deserved. England looked ragged, and their World Cup inability to produce in the second half gave little cause for optimism.

However, Sven must have said the right things at half time. England came out, sleeves rolled up and grafted. After 20 minutes they got a bit of luck and reward. Owen was the only one to react to Beckham's free kick and must have put the goalie off as he flicked his hair at it. As a striker Owen was forced to claim the credit although it was clear that he should not have and ultimately the goal went to Beckham. Nonetheless, Owen's contribution was vital. It was also much more tangible in the 82nd minute when he clearly did get his head to the ball and put England ahead.

England held on for three vital points in conditions which seemed to have little to do with international football. This impression was given further substance by the racist abuse which sections of the home support rained down on Emile Heskey and which saw UEFA take action against the Slovak FA. One way or another, England were just glad to have got out of town with what they came for. Four days later they were not so lucky.

Slovakia Quiz

(1) What are the two main clubs of beautiful Bratislava called?

(2) Which team won the 2003 Slovak Cup?

(3) True or false? The team in the previous answer was named after a soldier who fought with the forces of the Republic in the Spanish civil war and then stayed on afterwards to become a famous bullfighter and footballer with Sporting Gijon.

(4) In that cup final how many goals were scored in the space of how many minutes?

(5) Who was the only team Slovakia failed to score against in Euro 2004 qualifying?

(6) True or false? Most of the Slovak team play their club football in Slovakia.

Answers

1: Inter and Slovan 2: Matador Puchov 3: False. If for no other reason doubtful on the grounds that Franco would have had him shot 4: Three in five and all in extra time. 111 [Pernis for Matador Puchov], 115 [Hornyak equalised for Slovan], 116 [Breska nets the winner for Matador]. Some great names there! 5: Turkey to whom they lost 3-0 away and 1-0 at home 6: False, although in addition to those dotted around Europe, quite a few play in the Czech Republic

England 2 Macedonia 2 (Home — St Mary's Stadium, Southampton)

The contrast in venue and atmosphere could not have been greater four days after the Slovakia game. As we know, Southampton fans are the finest and (according to a University study) most tuneful in the land. Any right-wing urges were thus here channelled into versions of the national anthem. It always sounds a bit imperialistic to me, although the cricket Barmy Army's version (God Save YOUR Gracious Queen) to the Aussies has to be admired. In any case, the atmosphere was good as Southampton got the opportunity to host a full international for the first time in its new 32,000 stadium.

The pitch was also a stark contrast and could allow England no excuses. Not only was it immaculate, but St Mary's is the only completely flat pitch in the Premiership in the sense that its drainage system has no need of the usual slight camber. To describe the contrast between the pitch at Slovan's dilapidated stadium and that at St Mary's shiny new one would be to talk about the difference between something very smooth and something very very rough indeed. Perhaps the difference between Kim Wilde then and Kim Wilde now would give you some idea of the contrast. Bratislava's was as rough as the proverbial badger's arse, St Mary's as smooth as an Armani suit.

At the time, the suggestion was that England's 2-2 was a disaster. As it turned out England might have lost 3-0 and still qualified had all other results stayed the same. We should not forget also that Macedonia took the lead in plenty of other games, including twice in Turkey for which they got pelted by bottles (seems worse than a celebration to me, UEFA?). The fact that the Turks squeaked a 3-2 win and England did not is largely a matter of luck. It is significant that English 'spies' watching Macedonia train on the St Mary's pitch saw lots of shooting practice and very little defending.

In any case, just as the commentator was talking about how the Macedonians would have been happy to go 10 minutes without conceding, they were even happier to be 1-0 up. Seaman, already in the nation's collective bad-book for what was effectively a poor cross from Ronaldinho, flapped at an admittedly vicious swinging corner and the ball flew in the top corner. England looked nervous. Beckham, seeking an immediate way back on the pitch, hoofed the ball out of play, presumably trying to play in a striker who wasn't there.

But almost immediately it was Beckham who got England right back into it, bringing the ball down with what looked suspiciously like his arm and then floating a lob over a keeper caught out by his instant control. But England failed to relax and it was less than 10 minutes before Macedonia had retaken the lead. Gerrard gave the ball away very carelessly in mid-field and as a poor cross came in Sol Campbell was only able to clear weakly to the edge of the penalty area from where a clinical side-foot shot was dispatched around Seaman again.

Before half-time England had their equaliser. Good work by Beckham to keep the ball in play eventually saw a chance fall for Gerrard, who was able to make amends for

his earlier mistake by lashing home a half-volley after an excellent chest/thigh control. England went in at half-time in need of guidance from Sven and England fans hoped that the second-half World Cup malaise would not strike again. But strike it did.

In the second half play became increasingly compressed in the Macedonian half. Gerrard saw a delicate effort lob onto the roof of the net with the goalie in trouble. Jonathan Woodgate had a shot cleared off the line; surely had it fallen to a striker the defender on the line would have been avoided. Alan Smith, however, in for the injured Emile Heskey, didn't receive a chance of comparable ease, although of three half-chances falling his way a short-range falling volley went straight at the keeper when it could probably have gone anywhere.

In between those half-chances Smith displayed his youthful recklessness as he got a yellow card for a trade-mark and foolish lunge. Then as the match drew to a close a pointless tackle from behind when the ball was already out saw him yellow carded for the second time and hence sent off. I know the person likely to do an editing job on this is a Leeds fan so I'd just like to say that where Leeds fans see 'loyal' I see a 'liability'; where they see 'talented', I see 'tiresome'. That said I'd be quite happy for him to sign for Southampton [*In yer dreams! – Ed.*] and in the context of this match his sending off meant nothing.

A late break by Macedonia finished in a weak shot, but as already pointed out, if all other results had been the same England could have afforded to have lost this one anyway. So often in sport the losing player or team concentrates on their own performance. While there will always be some truth in this, we must also recognise that it has something to do with the opposition. Sven was right when he said 'We should win games like this and I'm sorry we didn't', but Macedonia deserved their result and deserved their celebration. Along with Greece and Turkey they are the only teams to take points off England in qualifying tournaments and I hope we can be as gracious about their efforts as the St Mary's crowd believe our Queen to be.

Macedonia Quiz

1. In how many of Macedonia's European qualifiers did they score the first goal?

2. Of these games, how many points did they get?

3. Of the games where Macedonia did not score first how did they get on?

4. True or false? Macedonia have always finished fourth in their qualifying group for major tournaments.

5. True or false? Macedonia is a part of Greece?

6. Why did Cementarnica count their blessings in the final of the Macedonian Cup final?

Answers

1: Five of eight games 2: Just two in away draws with Liechtenstein and England
3: Much better. Four points from just two games including a win against Liechtenstein and a
draw against Slovakia away 4: True 5: False. This one's a former Yugoslav Republic
6: After being pegged back from 3-1 to 3-3 they finally drew 4-4 [scoring an own-goal
equaliser for their opponents in the last 10 minutes] but then finally won 3-2 on penalties
after no goals in extra time. Blessing was also the scorer of their first goal

Intermission

In the gap between those two games the main talking points were the future of David Seaman, aged 39. He was not to finish the campaign. At the other end of the scale, Wayne Rooney was hardly heard of at the start of the campaign but very much a part of it by the end. Rooney's debut came in the friendly defeat by Australia. Many people were surprised by our defeat by Australia but not me; in a conversation with a Sydney taxi driver I had suggested a swap – a win at the SCG for England's cricket team in return for a win for the Socceroos in that one. It was agreed. He didn't care about the cricket as the Aussies were already 4-1 up and I don't care about friendlies.

Why should anyone care about friendlies? The constant encroachment by clubs on the legitimate demands of international football (although themselves legitimate when football has become such a business) mean that friendlies have to be experiments. Also I don't know if you have noticed but there are international teams which do seem to do OK in friendlies but never win tournaments – Colombia perhaps? If England turned it on and defended well in every friendly, every other team would have hours of video to look at to see how to beat us! So I am perfectly happy to see England swap and change in friendlies as long as we see the odd spark of inspiration and get the odd goal.

However, there is a theory of revolution which suggests that revolution happens not when people are at their most miserable and poor but when things have slightly improved for the better or when people can see some hope. Such was surely the case in Romania and other eastern bloc countries at the end of the 1980s. Interesting, by the way, that the west spent so much time protesting against communism and its 'elections' which allowed you to vote for only one candidate and now President Putin totally controls the media, openly talks of his disdain for genuine democracy and suspiciously arrests for corruption only those Russian billionaires who give money to the opposition...but then again Putin is open to foreign investment. That's by the by. My point was going to be related to how with football managers it can take only a slight downturn for their positions to look unsafe.

Perhaps the manner of England's exit from the World Cup didn't help. A freak goal and an inability – again in the second half – to create chances against 10 men. The nation, prepared for a party, got instead a rather resigned Eriksson saying that we'd done pretty well. We had, and perhaps defeat to Brazil saved us from the agony of losing in the final to Germany! But it did seem we'd rather gone with a whimper; lions in beating Argentina (which is worth mentioning again if you need to bring on the 'feel-good factor'), we were pussy-cats against their South American neighbours

But in any case, that defeat to Brazil, an unconvincing start to Euro 2004 qualifying and then a 3-1 defeat in an unimportant game (one in which we made 11 half-time substitutions *including* hardly established stars such as Ledley King and Francis Jeffers) seemed to mean that a 'Sven out' campaign was gaining momentum. After the Liechtenstein game (described below) you felt England were just one defeat from saying goodbye to Sven. Surely this shows how much madness is around? This is the man who took us to the World Cup when the whole country had virtually given up on the idea! Those who play any sport themselves will know it is impossible always to perform at your best, but that the great players – at whatever level – are able to produce the goods when it matters. Remember that if England lose to France in the opening game of 2004. It is unlikely I'll grant you, but it is not beyond the realms of possibility for England to lose that game and go on to beat France in the final! In any case, that is the context for the next series of games.

Liechtenstein O England 2 (Away – Rheinparkstadion)

As with almost all England games of the current era this game was preceded by a story other than about the match itself. It might be Sven's private life, the night-club antics of a player, missed drugs tests or whatever. On this particular occasion – because the whole world hates us for a century or so of imperialism followed up by support for US imperialism – it was terrorist threats. Tiny Liechtenstein, unable to cope, drafted in police from neighbouring Switzerland!

On the pitch things were much less dramatic. England didn't win 7-0 so the press said they weren't good enough. The things they said ought to have pressured Sven although, of course, he didn't show it. A header by Owen and a free-kick off the post by Beckham were enough. A late flurry by Liechtenstein seemed to boost the impression that England had under-performed...but again one must consider the proximity of the Turkey game just four days later. After the draw against Macedonia it became a 'must win' game, and unlike the 'must win' variety like Liechtenstein away, a much more difficult one to actually win.

Liechtenstein Quiz

(1) Why are Manchester United not good enough to win the Liechtenstein championship?

(2) But could Southampton win the Cup there?

(3) By what score did Vaduz win the 2003 Liechtenstein Cup final?

(4) In that game, Thomas Beck knocked in five goals. How many people were there to see the match?

(5) True or false? The number watching the 2003 Liechtenstein final was more than saw the 2002 Latvian final.

Answers

1: Because there isn't one. All the teams play in Swiss national and regional leagues
2: Possibly, although after that loss from 3-0 up against Tranmere the other year you never can tell. Also they'd have to go some to beat Liechtenstein giants Vaduz
3: They beat Balzers 6-0   **4:** 950   **5:** False. A whopping 1000 turned out to see Skonto Riga trounce Metalurgs 3-0

(6) How many recent cup finals around Europe have been watched by fewer than turn up for Vaduz?

(7) What remarkable thing happened on 30 April 2003?

(8) Hadn't that happened before?

(9) True or false? All the Liechtenstein national side play in either Liechtenstein or Switzerland.

(10) Before Macedonia came to England and took the lead before drawing in European qualifying, how had they got on in Liechtenstein?

Answers

6: At least one. 852 saw Barry beat Cwmbran 4-3 on penalties in Wales after a 2-2 draw and I couldn't find figures for Andorra, Faroes, and San Marino 7: Liechtenstein won, 1-0 in a friendly against Saudi Arabia 8: Yes actually. There are rumours of a similar success (2-1) versus Azerbaijan in 1997 9: False. Mario Frick plays in Italy for a team I've never heard of. He's the guy who almost got a late goal at Old Trafford 10: They took the lead before drawing, this time 1-1

England 2 Turkey 0 (Home – Stadium of Light)

What's the difference between the Stadium of Light in Sunderland and the new Estadio da Luz built for the finals and final of Euro 2004? I suppose the technical answer is the difference in capacity and the language of the name (which means the same). There are also similarities like the great atmosphere they create when full. But the comedy answer – which you can work up into a joke should you so wish – is that you've got more chance of understanding the locals in Lisbon. Moving swiftly on!

Turkey had before this match – and of course pleasingly at the time of writing – never scored against England. But also before this match no one was assuming that this record could automatically be preserved. Sven (perhaps responding to pressure, however unlikely that may seem) threw in Rooney for his full debut. The lad did not disappoint. Alpay – not picked for Villa all season – threw out the message to Graham Taylor that in this game he would see the real Alpay. If the real Alpay is a petulant tw*t then he did not disappoint.

The game started at pace. The Turks harried and irritated in response and Beckham was booked early for half an elbow which would keep him out of the next game at home to Slovakia. Then Gerrard did well to pull the ball back from the by-line. His high hanging cross was dropped by Rustu; Rooney's effort was well blocked and Beckham blasted wide with the goal at his mercy and in tap-in range. Thereafter Rustu makes amends; Rooney runs from the half-way line and clearly slides in Owen who seems to do nothing wrong but is thwarted by the keeper nonetheless.

England's chances are clear cut but few. In the second half quantity tends to increase at the expense of quality. Beckham's free-kick excites the crowd and worries the keeper as it slams into the side netting but never looks likely to have enough bend. Gerrard heads wide from a corner. A slight knock to Owen sees Vassell come on and look an instant threat, although he too is thwarted by Rustu. Another Beckham free-kick from Beckham is pushed wide. Vassell produces another save. It looks as though England might never score. Just 15 minutes remains.

And then Bridge (then a Saints player before being tempted by the dark side) puts in a fine cross. Initially the great chance which falls to Ferdinand is pushed out by Rustu (again!) but this time the rebound is slotted home under the keeper by Darius Vassell. How UEFA take the same view of booing a national anthem and a pitch celebration as they have of other things such as racist chanting I have no idea. I wonder if they will be on hand as God Save the Queen is played in Cardiff?

In any case, Turkey finally emerge now needing a goal and in their only proper effort Nihat (player of the year in La Liga no less) must have thought he'd scored, only for David James to leap acrobatically to his right to tip it around. After that Kieron Dyer loses his footing, does well to win the ball back and then loses his footing again in the area. The referee, presumably trying to give the score a look which reflects the match a little more, points to the spot. Surprisingly the Turkish team don't take it too well, but with the match already effectively won, Beckham blasts the ball into the corner for good measure.

Turkey Quiz

1. True or false? Turkey have finished third in their last two major tournaments?

2. Despite many impressive results in recent times, who performed against the Turks twice as well as England?

3. In qualifying England went behind to Macedonia three times. How many times did Macedonia take the lead against Turkey?

4. What is the name of the Turkish coach (although of course he might have been sacked by now)?

5. Which of the 'Big three' Turkish teams failed to qualify for Europe in 2003/04?

Answers

4: Senol Gunes   5: Fenerbahce

1: True. The World Cup of 2002 and The Confederations Cup of 2003

2: The Czech Republic beat them 4-0 in a friendly in April 2003   3: Also three

(6) Which team scored the most goals in the Turkish league in 2002/03?

(7) Who?

(8) Which team won the Turkish league that year and look likely to do it again in 2003/04?

Answers

6: Glencerbiligi with 76 from 34 games   7: The lot that dumped Blackburn Rovers out of the UEFA Cup   8: Besiktas

England 2 Slovakia 1 (Home – Riverside, Middlesbrough)

After another 'doesn't really tell you much' friendly against Serbia and Montenegro, the pre-match build-up here was all about the England captain, who wasn't playing. Reports were linking Beckham – swanning around the States somewhere I believe – with a move to Spain. Fortunately, it was England captain for the day – Michael Owen – who grabbed all the post match headlines on the occasion of his 50th cap; the youngest England player ever to achieve this milestone. Slovakia, needing to win to have any chance of qualifying for Euro 2004, were certainly in no mood to make things easy.

Despite this, Owen ought really to have scored for England after 60 seconds – the ball skimmed the goalie's thigh and went just wide for a corner. Thereafter the Slovaks were irresistible. They scored one (rather like Beckham's in Slovakia) and could have had at least two more in a first half that saw England in total disarray. So often in the World Cup England had failed to produce in the second half; now in qualifying they appeared to be doing the opposite and certainly needed to do the same again now. Sven didn't look worried. Well perhaps he did – a little!

Owen suggests that Sven put the team right at half time, precisely telling them what was going wrong and what they needed to do. Makes a change from previous managers. Can you imagine what Keegan said at half time in the last game at Wembley? Something like Mavis Riley – 'I don't really know Rita!' Anyway, it did look like Owen had been caught but with the ball possibly out of his control England can consider themselves a little fortunate to have got the penalty. But Owen made sure to take advantage of the luck.

Owen then scored a header from a fine cross from the lucky talisman Gerrard. Only a great save and the cross-bar prevented Owen from getting his hat-trick. Meanwhile Slovakia looked beaten, paying for their profligacy when they could have had the match sown up in the first half. England however failed to finish them off. Hargreaves and Gerrard both missed good chances to make victory more secure but in the end 2-1 was – and had to be – good enough. Wins against Macedonia and Liechtenstein would set up a final showdown in Istanbul with Turkey. But England had underestimated Macedonia once before – surely they would not do so again?

Macedonia 1 England 2 (Away – Gradski Stadium, Skopje)

Before travelling to Macedonia England trounced Croatia 3-1. Granted I have always said friendlies count for nothing but it would be nice if that could be repeated in the summer. Alas when it did come to the real thing again – and without travelling support – England did not start quickly like they had against Croatia. In fact, once again they had a poor first half, going behind as they did. Eriksson looked pretty close to annoyed. If he could only get the team to play for an entire match!

In a way, the new 'better in the second half' system is better, although slightly nerve-wracking. First, Rooney slotted home coolly to become the youngest ever goal-scorer for England. Then John Terry was brought down – no doubt about this one being a penalty – and Beckham slotted home from the spot. It is not a game which is likely to be remembered for much else. There was plenty of pre-game expectation in Macedonia, thanks largely to the 2-2 draw in England, but ultimately England got the three points they needed. Attention became more and more fixed on the Turkey v England fixture which would settle the group. Providing that is, England did the double over Liechtenstein. I'll put you out of your suspense...they did.

England 2 Liechtenstein 0 (Home – Old Trafford)

Although victory duly arrived against Liechtenstein, nobody really expected to have to wait until the second half again for England to play. However, with Sven (and England) much maligned after Macedonia at home, now looking for his eighth consecutive win to break Sir Alf Ramsey's record as an England manager, the away side battled tenaciously in the first half. Perhaps the national anthems – the same tune, different words – confused the teams. Certainly it was Liechtenstein who attacked first, although thereafter they had to rely on some outstanding goal-keeping.

Beckham, who had received an outstanding reception on his return to Old Trafford after moving to Real Madrid, hit the bar. I seem to remember Beattie hitting the bar but I might be getting my games confused! In any case it was 0-0 at half time. However, within a minute of the re-start nerves were settled; an excellent cross and a trademark run and stooping header by Owen gave England the lead. Barely five minutes later a fine cross-field pass from Owen to Beckham, led to Beckham's cross picking out Gerrard. As Gerrard looked to nod it back, Rooney moved into space and was able to control and lash the ball home with glee.

England relaxed. Beckham and Gerrard were subbed to ensure they did not get the yellow cards which would keep them out of the Turkey game, which was now the main topic of conversation. But Liechtenstein continued to hustle, without, it must be said, much real threat, although Frick's late run brought a smart save out of David James. England's wins against Liechtenstein had not been pretty but, for instance, the Germans had gone much closer to failing to take maximum points off the Faroe Islands. It would have been a waste to produce your big performances on occasions like these. We'll leave that sort of thing to the Spanish!

Turkey 0 England 0 (Away – Fenerbahce Stadium, Istanbul)

Before this one, England had won 11 of 13 qualifying matches under Sven. They had only lost competitively to the World Champions and had never conceded a goal to Turkey. Easy huh? Well of course no, especially when the only fans in the stadium for England were...well I'd better not tell you who they were, but where there's a will there's a way they say (although this required wit, intelligence and a command of foreign languages beyond that possessed by our hooligan element I suspect, so no problem).

In any case, the pre-match build-up had been all about

Rio Ferdinand and a missed drugs test rather than the match. This seemed to unite the players in some sense of misguided loyalty. I mean everyone knows how important these doping tests are; you don't just forget and if you do you should expect to face the consequences. In the event, John Terry deputised so well that Rio may struggle to get his place back.

In the game, Rooney almost opened the scoring, breaking through only to push his lob over an advancing Rustu but onto the roof of the net. Turkey however look a much more serious attacking proposition than the team which almost left Sunderland with a point. Even so, it was still England who looked the more threatening and it wasn't a surprise when Gerrard went down in the area and England earned a penalty. It looked fairly clear-cut but then again a referee less strong than Pierluigi Collina might have waved it away. His presence – as much as that of any referee could – reassured the millions watching at home on TV. Certainly Graham Poll would probably have booked Gerrard. He doesn't support Spurs by the way; simply any team playing against whoever I'm supporting!

Of course you are probably aware that Beckham set a new English record (originally set by Chris Waddle in 1990) for the biggest distance ever by which to miss a penalty kick, as he thrashed it a full 40 yards over the bar. Practising with Jonny Wilkinson wasn't such a good idea after all! Alpay of course ensured that the watching Graham Taylor saw the real Alpay. But still England pressed. Scholes tried to finish good work by Rooney, although as he shot narrowly wide many wished he'd left it to the youngster.

However, despite the fact England were playing well, and playing well in the first half, the longer it went on the more worried one became that England would ultimately pay for that penalty miss or that Collina would get one wrong. In a sense he did, not booking Suker (what a nice man) after a blatant dive in the area, but he at least did not award a penalty. Then Beckham does have the ball in the net, although it is disallowed for offside. Minutes later Dyer appears to be clean through; although Rustu spots the danger and rushes out to arrive at roughly the same time as Dyer, his head height challenge is appalling. It is reminiscent of Harald Schumacher flattening France's Battiston (was it?) in 1982 (was it?). However, Rustu's attempt to make what Tahar El Khalej did to Dyer look like a cuddle came to nothing: the keeper himself was fortunate to escape with a yellow card.

With seconds remaining we get a picture of the innocence of youth. With Turkey pressing and the score at 0-0, Wayne Rooney is smiling a smile which will be echoed in many living rooms up and down the country, but only in a few minutes time. At the death, a Nihat shot appears to be arrowing towards the top corner. It also appears to me to have taken the slightest of touches off Sol Campbell – enough to take it the wrong side of the post. The referee fails to give a corner and – for the benefit of viewers at home – England are able to celebrate on the pitch. Under Sven England have only rarely been pretty, but almost always effective. Subsequent friendly defeat against Denmark should, by now, not be fooling anyone. It's now time to see how we get on in the company of many of the top ranked teams in the world; they will be fearing us at least as much as we are worrying about them.

PS Latvia 1 Turkey 0, Turkey 2 Latvia 2. Latvia win 3-2 and qualify for the finals in Portugal 2004.

Chapter 3

The 2004 Championships – The Finalists

Introduction

This section analyses the recent form, history and team selection of the 16 finalists with some tentative predictions. In the conclusion, more specific predictions – based on the draw for the finals – will be made, so apologies if here I end up claiming that four teams will reach the final. The quizzes are divided into two halves, partly so you can recover with a piece of orange, if the mental energy expended on them is too great, or so you can play against someone else.

But First: The Rankings

This is a league table of the 16 qualifiers for Portugal 2004 and the five defeated play-off teams according to their FIFA World Ranking at the time of the end of the qualifying campaign. The number in brackets equals the FIFA world ranking.[6] Brazil were ranked first. Of course league tables are not always a good guide (Southampton 6 Man Utd 3 would be an example of where this is so) but for anyone outside the top 10 of this list to win would be a real shock and anyone outside the top six – with the possible exception of Portugal – a surprise.

FIFA Official World Rankings (at the end of October 2003)

[Eliminated play-off teams in square brackets]

1. France (2)
2. Spain (3)
3. Holland (5)
4. England (6)
5. Germany (7)
6. Italy (8=)
7. [Turkey (8=)]

---

[6] These rankings have thrown up some bizarre anomalies and given undue weight to some really unimportant matches, but they are – nonetheless – there or thereabouts.

8. Czech Republic (11)
9. Denmark (14)
10. Portugal (17)
11. Sweden (18)
12. Croatia (19)
13. Greece (26=)
14. Russia (28)
15. [Slovenia (29)]
16. [Norway (37)]
17. Bulgaria (39)
18. Switzerland (43)
19. [Scotland (58)]
20. [Wales (59)]
21. Latvia (69=)

Perspective

And this is a list of the European countries (and Israel who are in the qualifiers!) who, though they did not qualify for the play-offs or finals, are – according to FIFA – ranked above at least one of the 2004 finalists.

1. Republic of Ireland (15)
2. Belgium (16)
3. Romania (21)
4. Poland (26=)
5. Serbia and Montenegro (32)
6. Finland (41)

7. Israel (47)

8. Slovakia (49)

9. Ukraine (51)

10. Bosnia-Herzegovina (53)

11. Iceland (55)

12. Austria (62)

13. Hungary (67)

Other facts that may interest you before we look at the qualifiers in detail are:

1) Global cries for a merging of the home nations can only be strengthened by the news that only England – of the four – are ranked above Cuba (57).

2) Latvia's 69th place is shared with Burkina Faso.

3) England's opponents in the 2-2 qualifying draw at St Mary's (Macedonia) are ranked 91st equal with Albania, a full 85 places behind England.

4) With 204 teams in FIFA's rankings (propped up by Montserrat), Northern Ireland's 118th place means there are now only 85 teams actually worse than them. If they still haven't scored by the time you read this, expect a hastily-arranged friendly against Montserrat. But they must have scored by now...surely?)

5) The team Scotland huffed and puffed against to secure a play-off berth, Lithuania, are ranked 97th, amazingly nearly 40 places behind Scotland. Mind you, they did draw 1-1 in Germany, ranked 90 places above them too.

The Hosts: Portugal

In the immensely authoritative Arcturus *World Cup: Fact and Quiz Book* (2002), David Harding waxes lyrical: 'You can just picture it already: Alan Hansen and Mark Lawrensen talking inanely on a brightly coloured sofa discussing "dark horses" for the tournament. As quick as a Jamie Carragher-thrown coin into the crowd these two pundits look at each other and whisper "Portugal".' And nothing has really changed, except you might want to add something more topical than a Carragher coin throw. As quick as a Souness temper and hastily drawn conclusion perhaps? But unlike the 2002 World Cup – when clever-clogs Harding was able to predict a win for a team *speaking* Portuguese – this time surely they do have a chance as hosts, and probably as more than dark horses. Despite that, and especially as their neighbours Spain failed so badly when hosting the World Cup in 1982, there is less confidence, or even blind optimism, and more 'surely we've got to have a good tournament sometime haven't we?' about 2004.

For so many recent years the talk has been of the 'golden generation' fulfilling their potential. Portugal won the World Youth Cup of 1989 and 1991 and as a huge number of very talented young players became available for the national team over the next few years it was expected that Portugal would improve upon their almost pitiful international record. In the sense that Japan/South Korea was only Portugal's third World Cup finals they did – indeed – improve, but that tournament was the end of the

peak of the 'golden generation' who never, alas, became
the 'goal-den' generation. Faced with a group made up of
the hardly inspiring but efficient US team, the 'impressive in
qualifying' Poles and the eager – but surely lacking –
Koreans, the Portuguese probably felt that Poland were the
team to beat. However, they weren't, and after crashing
3-2 to the USA in a thrilling first game, Portugal reverted to
being dark cart horses of the tournament, eliminated via
their own appallingly negative tactics – and perhaps a little
bad luck – in defeat to South Korea. All that from a team
ranked 4 before the tournament. The 4-0 thrashing of the
even more disappointing Poles mattered not.

Expectations then of the 'golden generation' may have
receded, but expectation will still be very high because of
playing at home. The occasional appearance of Luis Boa
Morte in the team will not impress Southampton
supporters – whatever his efforts at Fulham – but the
Portuguese have many other good young players, including
Luis Figo who, despite looking craggy and ancient, will still
be only 31 by the time of the finals. Others to look for are
Fernando 'get yer 'air cut, son' Couto, Sergio Conceicao
and Pedro Pauleta.

Pauleta scored one of the goals as Portugal beat world
champions Brazil 2-1 in a friendly in March 2003. This win
can be added to others against Scotland, Bolivia,
Macedonia and away in Sweden. In fact, of a dozen
friendlies played whilst others were going about the
business of qualifying, the only one Portugal lost was away
to Italy 1-0. One thing which may not stand them in good
stead is that – with the exception of the Brazil game –

home fixtures have drawn pitifully small crowds. I mean surely the free-flowing and inspirational Scots deserved more than 8000? And although crowds for the final will clearly be higher, one wonders if such fans are likely to back the home team no matter what, or whether they will turn against them as quickly as David Pleat against Glenn Hoddle.[7]

Prediction

Host nations do not win major tournaments as often as you would think. Neither Belgium nor Holland won in 2000, with Belgium actually eliminated at the group stage despite playing more attractively than anyone in Belgium can ever remember. England fell at the semi-final stage in England in 1996, as did the Swedes themselves, at home in 1992 and West Germany back in 1988, so that one has to go back to France 1984 to find a home winner. On the other hand there have been a lot of semi-finalists, including 2000 where co-hosts Holland reached that stage. And Portugal are a talented team. Even Mexico as World Cup host nation has reached the quarter-finals in both 1970 and 1986.

All in all however, Portugal do not have a winning 'mindset'; others like France do; Germany always make the best of what they have; England have lost only one

---

[7] This comment refers to criticism of Hoddle by Pleat, which Hoddle suggests undermined him at Spurs. Since Hoddle was sacked after seeing his team comprehensively thrashed at home by Southampton others might consider the criticism somewhat justified. Since Hoddle had previously left the Saints after they gave him the chance to re-launch his career, still others, who believe in that sort of thing, might see it as some sort of judgement...

competitive fixture under Sven (admittedly to Portuguese speakers). In other words, it would be a big surprise if Portugal did not get beyond the initial group stage but an even bigger one, despite home advantage, if they actually won.

Semi-finalists.

A Quiz of Two Halves

First Half

(1) Before hosting this year's tournament, Portugal had qualified for more World Cups than European Championships. True or false?

(2) Tottenham Hotspur superstar Helder Postiga (things will need to have changed by the time of publication of course for that phrase to sound OK) scored twice in his first full match for Portugal after a couple of sub-appearances. Who was the match against?

(3) Somewhat bizarrely,[8] the sentence 'Liar liar my a-knobs on fire' contains the names of two Swiss referees who refereed consecutive games of Portugal in April 2003. True or false?

(4) True or false? The Norwegian referee of Portugal's friendly in England in September 2002 was called Odd Bent Ovrebo?

Answers

1: False. Portugal have qualified for three World Cups and three European Championships. The fact that they qualified for Euro 96 and Euro 2000, as well as the World Cup in 2002, means that in this context perhaps the 'golden generation', really have produced the goods after all! 2: Bolivia 3: True. On 2 April Herr Nobs refereed a 1-0 victory over Macedonia in a friendly played in Switzerland. Then on 30 April Herr Meier refereed a Portuguese friendly in Eindhoven against Holland 4: Actually I do not know Mr Ovrebo's first names but Odd and Bent are perfectly acceptable names in Norwegian so it's entirely possible I guess

[8] Perhaps as bizarrely as me thinking of this question!

Second Half

(5) Fulham's – and former Southampton player – Luis Boa Morte has been capped at international level about as often as Matthew Le Tissier. True or false?

(6) Which two Portuguese players will be hoping to reach, or to have just reached, 100 caps by the time of the finals?

(7) Who scored both Portugal's goals in a comfortable 2-0 win over Scotland in November 2002?

(8) Which team were Portuguese Champions in 2002/03?

(9) Which team won the Portuguese Cup final in 2002/03?

(10) Who was Portugal's player of the year in 2002/03?

Answers

5: Outrageously true! **6:** Fernando Couto and Luis Figo **7:** Pauleta **8:** FC Porto **9:** FC Porto, who beat Uniao Leira 1-0 **10:** Naturalised Brazilian Deco, playing for, inevitably FC Porto. Deco is beginning to break into the national team

Always Look On The Bright Side of Life: Denmark

Twenty years ago the Danes, in footballing terms, were hardly even regarded as highly as, say, Finland are today. They finished bottom of qualifying group 1 for Italy 1980, behind Bulgaria, Eire, Northern Ireland and England. And yet, four years later, in a group with England again, they won at Wembley and pipped England by a point to qualification. Perhaps amazed by it all, Danish fans decided to regard success as an excuse to party, and with their flag the opposite of England's (white cross, red background) have become a mirror image of England in so many respects, both on, but more especially off, the pitch.

Historically expectations of the Danish team are low and so success is relatively easy to achieve in this context. The fans are male and female and about as intimidating as a very fluffy bunny rabbit on a very fluffy (possibly pink or pale yellow) pillow, although considerably noisier it must be admitted. Rumour has it, in fact, that if you play 'God Save the Queen' backwards it is actually 'Let's all have a disco' in Danish. Hanging on for a draw in Bosnia to qualify for 2004 was not too inspiring, but the Danes proved themselves a decent side by winning at Old Trafford in a rare defeat for Sven's men.

But back in 1992 Denmark produced the most remarkable performance in European Championship history. Failing to qualify for the tournament in neighbouring Sweden was presumably a disappointment to players and fans alike, but also – one suspects – something which was kept very much in perspective too. However, with Yugoslavia ousted from the tournament for political reasons, in stepped the Danes; returning at short notice from the beaches of southern France and wherever else, the Danes made a mockery of the idea of preparation, playing fantastic – and steadily improving – football ultimately to overcome the (it was them again) Germans in the final.

Denmark's team today has some familiar faces and – unlike the days when England losing to Denmark would have been a big shock – these days it is a bit like, say, Charlton winning against Liverpool. You feel that England/Liverpool should win, but then again you have to confess that Charlton have got some good players whose team work might just swing it. Fortunately, and despite the friendly game in November 2003, such was not the case in Japan as England eased home 3-0 in the rain – but it could have been.

Talking of Charlton, one of the best known names in the Danish team – at least in England – would be Claus Jensen, along with Niklas Jensen of Manchester City. In goal they have Thomas Sorensen, lucky not to be credited with Rio Ferdinand's World Cup goal. Thomas 'is it Lee Carsley?' Gravesen of Everton and Jesper 'I'm afraid we can afford better players than you now' Gronkjaer of Chelsea will also feature. Newcastle fans will remember with a grimace Jon Dahl Tomasson, although he has fared much better in Italy. Per Frandsen of Bolton doesn't get much of a look-in these days. Peter Lovenkrands looks pretty good against the likes of Motherwell and Partick Thistle.

Quite a few Danes play, like Tomasson, in Italy, including Helveg and Laursen, and in other European countries too. Sharing the goal-scoring duties with Tomasson will be Dennis Rommedahl who plays in Holland and Ebbe Sand who plays for Schalke 04 in Germany. Poulson is also at Schalke. There are a couple of Danes playing for Panathinaikos as well as several still playing for FC Copenhagen, Brondby, Odense or Aalborg. Peter Skov-Jensen plays for the superbly named Midtjylland...who are ya?

Prediction

After surprising the football world by qualifying at England's expense back in 1984, Denmark's record in European Championships has been remarkable. They were actually the worst team at the finals in 1988 and 2000 and were disappointing in 1996, and yet in the only tournament they didn't qualify for, they were invited as guests and romped home by beating Germany in the final – and not just the shadow of a Germany we see over 10 years later but the World Cup holders. In *The World Cup 2002: Fact and Quiz Book* I confidently predicted that the USA had no chance by using the words 'zip, zero, zilch, nada'. But some inspired play and being in the 'reserves' half of the draw meant that they were quarter-finalists. So, whilst I would be very surprised by Danish success, neither is it something I would rule out. About the same level of probability as Southampton getting to an FA Cup final.

Eliminated at group stage, subject to the 'Carlsberg Clause' (i.e. 'probably').

A Quiz of Two Halves

First Half

1 How many games in a row did Denmark win before drawing against Romania at home in European qualifying?

2 In that draw, when did the Danes equalise, in effect smoothing their path to European qualification?

3 Does Stig Tofting, half-man, half-rottweiler, still play for Denmark?

4 Are all Danish midfielders required to shave their heads as part of some crazy Viking ritual?

5 Denmark qualified for Euro 2004 after securing a vital 1-1 draw away to the footballers formerly known as parts of Yugoslavia. But who scored for the Danes in the home match against the very same Bosnians and Herzegovinians?

Answers

5: Nobody, as they lost 2-0

1: Eight   2: The fifth minute of injury time   3: Apparently not   4: Apparently so

Second Half

6 Which famous former player currently coaches Denmark?

7 Who won the Danish Championship in 2002/03?

8 Who won the Danish Cup final in 2002/03?

9 In 2003/04 which teams replaced relegated Silkeborg and Koge?

10 Did you really expect us to know that one?

 Answers

6: Morten Olsen – he's famous in Denmark, OK? 7: FC Copenhagen 8: Brøndby, who beat Midtjylland 3-0 9: Herfølge and Frem 10: No, sorry!

Rubbish, But Don't Write Us Off: Germany

Absolutely typical I guess. Germany were playing away to the Faroe Islands in qualifying and were drawing 0-0. The added time board was being adjusted and the locals were beginning to nudge each other nervously. Having beaten Germany reserves (Austria) in their first ever European Championship game (1-0) the Faroes awaited an even bigger celebration. Then up pops Klose (which would have allowed some good *Sun* headlines if they could have been bothered) and Bobic in the 89th and 90th minutes. Germany 2-0 Faroe Islands; the score-line looks comfortable. It is a typically German 'effort' and why, even in these days of beating them 5-1 in Munich,[9] all England fans await games against Germany with a mixture of expectation, hope and fear.

If Portugal is reaching the end of its golden generation, Germans will be looking to 2004 to signal the end of its 'not quite good enough' generation, just in time for the World Cup 2006 which they controversially host ahead of South Africa and England (who held it last eight years before Germany last did in 1974). Although in the past we might look back on German teams and see an awesome array of powerful forwards, intelligent midfielders, imposing defenders and 'why did he punch that?' goalies, today it seems we merely see a team which is quite good. The fact

[9] 1 September 2001: Finger-wagging Jancker 6, Owen 13, 48, 66, Gerrard 45, Heskey 74.

that they were slightly peeved about Owen Hargreaves declaring himself English seems to confirm that.[10]

However, what characterises Germany down the years is not, necessarily, the great players and great teams. They have never captured the imagination in the way that Holland, Italy and Brazil have done (although the latter less often than the mythology would imply). No, what has characterised Germany is the ability to make the best of themselves. This is exemplified by Japan/Korea. We can moan all we want about the lucky Germans (oh don't worry, we will) and the fact that they didn't meet any kind of serious opposition until the final (promptly losing to them more heavily than England had when playing badly) but the fact is the Germans made the final.

Before that tournament I ran some comments past a German friend; 2002 was about restructuring for the Germans; they went to the World Cup without serious hopes and ambitions. He agreed. And yet they were not an outrageous amount of luck from upsetting the Brazilians. A German team without high expectations and without an enormous amount of talent nonetheless reached the final.

Late equalisers and penalty shoot-out wins seem to typify the German spirit which, at least from the outside, manifests itself not as plucky determination under pressure but cold, aloof superiority. It is what Portugal don't have. It is what Spain don't have. It can be exemplified most easily

[10] Actually Owen's quite good; this sentence included to cheer up the 43 Canadian soccer fans.

by something which happened half a century ago, in the 1954 World Cup in Switzerland. Having lost 8-3 to the undisputed best team (Hungary) in an earlier round, the Germans still went on to beat them 3-2 in the final. Although in 1966 and 1976 the Germans lost finals of tournaments (England 4-2 after extra time and against the Czechs on penalties) on both occasions they had scored last-minute equalisers even to take the game into the extra period.

One of the most fascinating things I have read about the Germans was a survey which compared the alcohol consumption allowed by players of the various national teams in Euro 96. Many, I think England amongst them, were officially banned from alcohol consumption during the tournament, whilst others, one supposes, were allowed a glass of wine with meals. However, top of the boozing league, with two bottles of beer per day – preferably after training – were the *Deutscher Meister* who went on to win the tournament after depressingly coming from behind to beat the hosts, as they had done also on at least two other occasions.

Many of the German team play in Germany with a wider range of clubs represented than the relatively few teams which go to make up the England team, even if Sven has opted to choose the occasional player from Charlton or Southampton.[11] In recent times, international appearances have been made by players from Dortmund, Hamburg,

[11] Actually this turns out not to be true, such is the extent to which Sven has handed out new caps in friendlies and to players outside the big clubs. See England section.

Leverkusen, Bochum, Bayern Munich, Kaiserslautern, Schalke 04, Bremen, Hertha Berlin, Hanover, Wolfsburg, 1860 Munich and Stuttgart! Overseas teams – like England in recent times – have been few and far between in terms of representing Germany. Arsenal's impressive – though not always in a good way – juggler in chief Jens Lehmann and Liverpool's Dietmar Hamann are among the names likely to be most familiar. With two players from England having been represented in recent squads this makes England the overseas country to have contributed most players to the German team. This is hardly surprising when 13 German teams have been represented with Bayern, Bremen, Leverkusen and Dortmund contributing several players each.

Prediction

So, even in decline, Germany managed to reach the World Cup final in 2002, and though hardly impressive – or stretched – in qualifying, I guess we really cannot anticipate that they will roll over for anyone this time, more than any other time. If they get the right draw and a bit of luck they might make the semi-finals...at which point you wonder if they might make the final...and so on. All of that said, I can't see Germany lifting the trophy.[12]

Surprise Semi-Finalists.

[12] In fact, should a situation arise where they reach the final I would probably only watch Germany play if it was against England. And if they were to win that game I don't think the TV would remain on for the presentations. So not only can't I see the Germans winning, I absolutely refuse to!

A Quiz of Two Halves

First Half

1. 'What is green and smells of fish?' – although in German obviously – is a German football song. True or false?

2. 'Take those little leather shorts off.' – although in German obviously – is also a German football song. True or false?

3. Germany struggled with two last minute goals to win their away qualifier against the Faroes (124th in the world). Did they also struggle in the home leg?

4. Why can we say that Germany had a 'close' shave in both games versus the Faroes?

5. So what happens when they come up against decent opposition then?

 Answers

1: True, a song of 'tribute' from Bayern fans to Werder Bremen   2: True, this being Bremen's frightening retort to the fish jibe above   3: Yes, it was 1-1 at half time and they scraped home 2-1   4: The winning goal in Germany *and* the go-ahead goal away were both scored by Miroslav Klose   5: Well apart from taking the opportunity to gratuitously mention the 5-1 match of 1 September 2001, in Germany's next two games after the Faroes home fixture they lost 3-1 to Holland (home) and then 3-1 to Spain (away) with Bobic grabbing a consolation on each occasion

Second Half

6 How many German players are called Fritz or have 'von' in their name?

7 OK, that question about promotion and relegation in Denmark was a bit unfair. How about naming me one of the teams who replaced Arminia Bielefeld, Nurnberg and Energie Cottbus in the Bundesliga in 2003/04?

8 Bayern Munich did the double in 2002/03. How easy was it?

9 In 2002/03 which drew the bigger crowd, the English Cup final, the German one or the Italian?

10 Michael Ballack moved for the 2002/03 season from terminal runners-up Bayer Leverkusen (nicknamed Neverkusen) to Bayern Munich. In his first season Bayern were unstoppable and he was the best player in Germany. But how did his old pals at Leverkusen get on without him?

Answers

6: None, so stop your stereotyping. **7:** You could have had Freiburg, Koln (Cologne) or Eintracht Frankfurt. **8:** Very. They took the league by 16 points from nearest rivals Stuttgart and were 3-0 up in the Cup against 10 men with 10 minutes to go. They cruised home 3-1 in the end against Kaiserslautern. **9:** Italy 76,000, England over 73,000, Germany just over 70,000. Although the Italian Cup Final is over two legs – the first leg attracted around 60,000 with the second leg being the 76,000. **10:** They finished fourth bottom and narrowly avoided relegation.

Nice Shirts, Shame About the Hair: Italy

How pleased were *you* by Italy's controversy-riddled exit from the World Cup? Marvellous, eh? I say this partly to annoy one particular Man U supporter I know, who I refer to as Man U to annoy several Man U fans I know. But also because don't the Italians just take themselves *far* too seriously?[13] It's the old 'you used to be a big club' syndrome, made famous by Nottingham Forest fans, but applied to the international scene. These days they are 'quite good' I'll grant you but despite a tolerable tournament record they're nowt but a team of hatchet style butchers and diving prima donnas who at various points have been outshone by either England, Germany or France at international level and who currently wouldn't even be favourites against Spain, Portugal or England – and maybe not even Wales against whom they got their qualifying campaign off to such an inauspicious start.

OK, OK that may be a little harsh, but there is a little of the 'God given right' about Italy, whose fans are prone to the same delusions as England fans in believing their team to be the very best in the world – whatever mere statistics say! True, they almost did, and should have, won Euro 2000 and if I'm honest (which is a rare characteristic of anyone writing about football) then they probably do have a better record than England. But if ever another country was going to sing about 'oh so nears' it is this one. They

[13] Exemplified by Perugia's threat to sack their Korean player for being rubbish all season and then knocking them out of the World Cup!

lost on penalties in World Cup 1994 after a 0-0 bore draw versus Brazil; Roberto Baggio's spot kick miss allowing the altogether more modest talents of Dunga to lift the cup. And, in 1990, on a seemingly unstoppable course to the final as host nation, stumbled over Argentina despite taking the lead. However, when they get it right – as they did superbly in 1982 – they really are unstoppable. Perhaps a return to the Iberian peninsular of that triumph will inspire them this time.

Like Germany, Italy has a squad made up of players from a wide variety of home-based players. The following teams have provided players for the national team in the recent past: Juventus, Roma, Internazionale, AC Milan, Lazio, Atalanta, Chievo, Bologna, Empoli, Parma and Perugia. This list of 11 isn't quite as extensive as the 13 home-based clubs who have provided players for Germany but it ain't bad. In fact scanning down the list for players earning a living abroad who have turned out for Italy recently and we find just the rather hopeless Massimo Maccarone of Middlesbrough who has so far picked up just two caps. Given three other Massimos in the squad perhaps it's a case of mistaken identity.

At the time of writing, Italy's form in 2003 has been impressive in both friendlies and European qualifiers. Although they did drop a point away to Serbia and Montenegro, this form was more than enough to see them comfortably home as group winners after they had initially struggled, with defeat in Cardiff and a home draw against the self same Serbia and Montenegro (at the time playing as Yugoslavia, I believe).

Prediction

Italy are often uninspiring in a tournament's early stages. In 1982 they failed to win any group matches at all but went on to lift the cup. In 1996, although winning their first game, they were then eliminated, many believe through complacency. And so, much will depend on whether the Italians negotiate their group. If they do – and depending on how the draw works out – they are potential finalists as much as England.

Semi-final at least.

A Quiz of Two Halves

First Half

(1) Italy's recent home friendlies – for instance v Slovenia, Turkey, Portugal and Northern Ireland – averaged more or less than 20,000 attendance?

(2) At the time of writing (19.24 on 5 November 2003) who was the last player to score for Italy whose name does not end in a vowel?

(3) Who on earth is Akhmedov?

(4) Oh that's just cheating isn't it?

(5) OK then, are there any players in the Italian team whose names do NOT end in a vowel?

Answers

1: Slightly less   2: Akhmedov   3: He scored an own-goal in Italy's favour while turning out for Azerbaijan   4: Yes it is   5: Yes, Buffon...but he plays in goal

127

Second Half

6 Who scored most goals and in most matches for Italy during qualifying?

7 Who was second top scorer in Italy in 2002/03?

8 Which player scored three goals in the Italian Cup final of 2002/03 and was still on the losing team?

9 How many teams get relegated from Serie A and how?

10 Name a team promoted to Serie A for the 2003/04 season?

Answers

6: Filippo Inzaghi scored six including a hat-trick against Wales but only found the net in three games. Del Piero's five goals were scored in four games. **7:** One Adrian Mutu, then of Parma. **8:** Totti, who scored once in the first leg defeat and twice in the second leg draw **9:** Four. The bottom three plus the losers of a play-off between the teams placed fourth and fifth bottom. In 2002/03 Regina beat Atalanta 2-1 in this play-off **10:** You could have Siena, Sampdoria, Lecce or Ancona

Was 2002
Just a Blip?: France

Despite Japan/Korea 2002 France will go into these European
Championships buoyed up by an absolutely outstanding run
of results. After trailing 1-0 for 25 minutes in Cyprus in the
first qualifying match and barely escaping with a 2-1 win
many were suggesting that France's day was done. However,
they won the remaining qualifiers – all seven – scoring 27
more goals and conceding just one. They also bagged the
Confederation Cup and not since Tunisia just after the last
World Cup has anyone really looked like beating them.[14] So
what of their chances this time and what of my right to judge?
Well, I was somewhat non-committal before the tournament
(in Japan/Korea) but did predict Senegal to produce the
biggest shock and they didn't let me down.

Perhaps a sign of French strength – although more likely
that their domestic game is not very good – is that whereas
most German players play in Germany, the Italians in Italy
and the English in England, the French are spread out
though Europe's best leagues: England is perhaps the most
popular destination (you complain about the food but
you're happy to take the money then!) with 12 recent
French players playing mostly for Manchester United or
Arsenal, but others too. England is followed by Spain
(three), Italy (five) and Germany (two). Fourteen players

---

[14] This is NOT actually true! They lost 2-0 at home to the Czech Republic on 12
February 2003 but so unlikely a result was this that in research I actually
recorded the score the wrong way round. A bit like that time when the papers
assumed England had beaten the USA 10-1, although different.

who have played in recent games play in France but many of these only occasionally or as substitute.

The novelty of success hasn't worn off for the French with international friendlies attracting crowds in excess of 50,000 on a regular basis, and as a nation which produces an irritating range of sporting success at other sports such as rugby and tennis, they will be hopeful again in Portugal. On paper, at least, nothing should stop a team who could field Barthez, Silvestre, Gallas, Desailly, Petit, Viera, Makelele, Wiltord, Cheyrou, Pires and Henry just from its recent English-based players. But let's face it, this is a country without footballing tradition, history or passion; as ever it would be a shame for them to win. And as my wife – looking over my shoulder as I write – points out, what this book really needs is more stuff about how really super England are. So that's your lot on France.

Prediction

On the grounds that I am hopeless at predictions, I predict France to get to the final, although alas I mean it. No other team seems capable of putting together such fluent football. At best they seem a wonderfully oiled machine. However, on the flip side, when the oil runs low they do seem to misfire badly allowing hope for other teams. They fired at the right time in France 1998, despite near elimination by Paraguay, and they fired at the right time (and with no little luck) in Euro 2000. This time expect class to carry them to the final and luck to finally run out (hopefully against England).

Finalists.

A Quiz of Two Halves

First Half

(I) In the twelve months from 12 October 2002 to 11 October 2003 in what percentage of their games did France find the net three times?

(2) In what percentage did they not concede a goal?

(3) Despite conceding only two goals in qualifying, France in fact trailed in two games in European qualification. One was in the 2-1 win in Cyprus. When was the other occasion?

(4) In what percentage of European qualifiers did Thierry Henry find the net and how many times was that in total?

(5) Was Thierry Henry France's top scorer in European qualification then?

Answers

1: 60%   2: 80%   3: They went 1-0 down to Israel away, on that occasion also coming back to win 2-1   4: 50%, six goals   5: Yes and No. Sylvain Wiltord also bagged six

Second Half

(6) Who takes France's penalties?

(7) True or false? The French Cup final of 2002/03 drew a higher crowd than the English and German equivalents and more than either leg of the Italian version.

(8) Did they get their money's worth?

(9) Who were French champions in 2002/03?

(10) True or false? Le Havre finally got relegated in 2002/03?

Answers

6: Against Malta Zidane, against Colombia Henry and against Japan Pires – apparently
7: True: 78,316   8: After Hugo Leal had given PSG the lead, he then proceeded to get sent off in the second half. Auxerre then pressed with the extra man, equalising in the 77th minute and netting the winner in the last. So, yes, probably   9: Lyon   10: True

Neither, I Want It For My Armpits: Sweden

Ah, the arrogant Swedes...or at least to their neighbours the traditional regional super power is regarded thus, although unlike the English, Sweden was rather quicker at giving other people their countries back rather than inventing the United Kingdom of Scandinavia and Southern Finland...[Editor's Note: Is this actually relevant? No? Well get on with it then!] OK, OK, I was only setting the context as Sweden being a bit like Nottingham Forest – you know, you used to be a big club. You'd think I'd know better than this living in Nottingham but as far as I'm concerned, there's only one team in Nottingham and that's County. Actually if 'You Pies' have folded by the time you read this, there might only be one team in Nottingham...let's hope not eh...that would be a disaster. [Editor's Note: I'm warning you, this is supposed to be about bloody Sweden!]

OK, it is thought that the area currently known as Sweden was settled by nomadic herdsmen from Europe escaping hordes moving in from the Russian Steppes as early as 3000 BC...[Editor's Note: Right! Do you know *anything* about Swedish football?] Of course, only kidding...keep yer hair on son. They are one of many sporting nations to begin with the letter S – Slovenia, South Africa and Senegal to name but a few – and got to the World Cup final in 1958 and reached the semi-finals and came third in 1994. They last lost to England in 965. [Editor's note: He *might* mean 1965 rather than 965 but it's difficult to be sure; it *was* a long time ago!]

Two things confuse people most about Sweden, apart from their rich history and political structures which apparently this editor is not interested in. One is, why have they got it in for Poland? In qualifying for Euro 2000 they beat Poland twice, including the game which saw England sneak into the play-offs because of their superior record versus the Poles. Then in qualifying for Portugal they beat Poland twice and then lost at home to Latvia when victory would have seen the Poles themselves qualify for the play-offs by virtue of their head-to-head record v Latvia! The second thing is why Anders Svensson looks so bloody good for Sweden but never really seems to fulfil his potential in a Saints shirt. Irritating that.

A large number of players have represented Sweden in recent times, which suggests more about experimentation than a surfeit of talent. Many of these players play abroad, but also many for clubs which sound unfamiliar even after years of following European football: Djurgardens? Orgryte? Landskrona? Sundsvall? Everton?! Many others play for the established Swedish giants like Malmo, AIK Stockholm or Halmstads or in neighbouring Denmark and Norway. Dotted around Europe you will also find the odd Swede – and in Freddy Ljungberg's case a very odd Swede – in Scotland, England, Portugal, Germany, France and Holland. By far the best of these is Michael 'Killer' Svensson of Southampton, although again how one can be so accurate with defensive headers and then miss the chances he has, is baffling! [Editor's Note: Apart from Southampton having a couple of Swedes, I'm still not convinced he knows very much about Sweden at all. So for all the information you need, please consult *www.svenskfotboll.se*, where you'll find all the latest news, facts and figures – in Swedish I'll grant you...]

Predictions

By now we have come to expect Sweden to have a good team but not a very good team. Even when they exceed expectations, however, we never really think they will be quite good enough. So it will be again this time, although they do have the talent to reach the quarter-finals and once there anything can happen. If you want to pin me down – and I think the editor's beginning to twig that I'm making this up – then I'd go for group stage elimination.

Eliminated at group stage. Quarter-finalists on a good day. Semi-finalists on a very, very good day. Finalists on an exceedingly good day. Winners on the kind of day when you stuff the millions you just won betting on seven at the casino in your pocket, climb into your sleek hundred and seventy grand Ferrari, drive back to your penthouse suite with your super-model girlfriend and just as she's slipped into her sexiest underwear seven of her mates arrive asking if they can join in...so an unbelievably good day in other words.

A Quiz of Two Halves

First Half

1. True or false? Sweden was settled by nomadic herdsmen from Europe escaping hordes moving in from the Russian Steppes as early as 3000 BC.

2. True or false? If the editor wanted a serious football book he should have stumped up some more cash and got Brian Glanville or someone to write the book?

3. But do you think they'd have got anyone else to do it for the same cash in virtually no time at all?

4. Is Skoog the name of a rather ornate lamp available at Ikea or the player who scored Sweden's goal on 18 February 2003 in a 1-1 draw with North Korea?

5. The game referred to in the question above was in something called the King's Cup. On 22 February the same teams contested the final. What was the score and how many did old Skoogy-doo bag himself this time?

Answers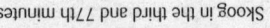

1: Unless it was a very lucky guess, false   2: True   3: Precisely my point   4: I would hope you'd heard of Niklas Skoog of Malmo   5: Sweden 4-0 North Korea including goals by Skoog in the third and 77th minutes

Second Half

(6) Who top-scored for Sweden in qualifying?

(7) Who won the 2002 Swedish Championship?

(8) Who won the Swedish Cup in 2002?

(9) True or false? One time giant IFK Gothenburg were relegated in 2002.

(10) Who top-scored in the Swedish league at almost a goal a game?

Answers

6: Marcus Allback with five **7:** Djurgardens held off many more famous clubs such as Malmo **8:** Bloody hell, it was Djurgardens again with a 1–0 golden win against AIK **9:** False but only just. As the third bottom team in the top division they had to win a play-off against the third top team from the division below **10:** Peter Ijeh of Malmo got 24 in a 26-game season

Representing All That Is Good and Decent in The World: England

How can you lie there and think of England when you don't even know who's in the team – *Billy Bragg*

Something that every football fan knows; it only takes five fingers to form a fist – *Billy Bragg*

You could intellectualise these quotes if you will, as some kind of comment on the dominance of hegemonic masculinity amongst England fans – and good luck to you if you know what that means any more than I do – but I put them there mainly because it's the sort of thing we authors do, and also because you really should go and dig out those old Billy Bragg records, or even update your collection with a CD purchase. They're surprisingly catchy *and* you can sing at least as well as he can.

Returning to football and the section title, despite a history of colonialism which has often caused the English to take this self-view – although one ought to add that the Scots *were* disproportionally represented in the British Empire – it is not one which is widely held. And whilst our current role as arch-apologists for the United States evil global project [Editor's note: You should be thankful we restricted him to that! We had to delete all sorts of 'US is a terrorist state', 'human rights abusing hypocrite' stuff!] may make us even less popular, it is really the reputation of our football supporters which Saatchi and Saatchi would have most trouble putting a positive PR gloss on. Even so, it does seem like a self-fulfilling prophecy in which England attracts dick-heads. I find those 'diary of a hooligan' books a bit tedious, but there's plenty out there if you want to research this assertion.

In short, England has a very good team, an excellent 'fighting' record[15] in competitive football and it really would be a crying shame if all that was jeopardised this time, more than any other time and so we'd better hope the authorities find a way, find a way to stop the fighting etc. Travel in Europe does not inspire one with confidence (we Saints fans are experts after a trip to Romania!). Intelligent policing seems to be replaced by the 'maximum number of riot police theory' tried and tested (to destruction) in Italy and Argentina, for instance.

Anyway, England does have an exceptional array of talent, well managed, although how any of that explains Francis Jeffers and Paul Konchesky having an England cap I don't know. Jamie Carragher has more England caps than Matt Le Tiss!? I guess if friendlies in his day had been used to involve changing the entire team every 15 minutes we might have seen the God-like one in an England shirt more often? Anyway, with talent available down the middle with Campbell at centre-half, with Beckham in midfield and

---

[15] By 'fighting record' I don't mean that they fight but that they are good at coming from behind. Oh, and by 'good at coming from behind' I don't mean...[Editor's note: Censored]

Owen up front, if other players can come through we must have a real chance.

As with the past, most England players play in England. The fate of Steve MacManaman may have dissuaded others from going abroad, although if David Beckham impresses the Spaniards with his work rate *and* skill as he appears to be doing, others may feel inclined to follow suit. Sven has changed a little the days when England teams picked Arsenal's defence, Manchester United's midfield and Liverpool's attack plus Emile Heskey. In fact, when I began writing this, and in view of the old Man U, Arsenal, Liverpool (with a Leeds sub) selection process, I thought Germany's record of having 13 Bundesliga teams represented at international level in recent times was quite exceptional. I was also impressed with Italy's 11 although I did know that many more English teams now provide players for the national squad. In fact, in recent times players from Manchester United, Liverpool and Arsenal, obviously, but also West Ham, Leeds, Middlesbrough, Southampton, Blackburn, Chelsea, Newcastle, Aston Villa, Tottenham, Charlton, Birmingham *and* Everton have all represented England! That's 14 Premiership teams and one West Ham.

At the World Cup England showed promise, especially when before Sven took over we had lost at home to Germany and drawn away to Finland such that even qualification looked a long way off. England had then won in Germany 5-1 (did I mention that?) and showed that fighting spirit in securing the point needed against Greece. Again in qualifying England were impressive (see separate chapter) recovering from deficits in many qualifying games and holding on to 0-0 in Turkey despite having no fans.

Prediction

England will be – without a shadow of a doubt – one of the best teams at the tournament, with only France being of the calibre you would expect to defeat England more often than not. Accordingly, given the manager we were denied in 1992 and 2000 and the luck denied in 1996 we should really go all the way.

Finalists. Possibly winners (though much will depend on Campbell, Beckham and Owen, we also need Calamity James to continue error free, Bridge to oust the liability Ashley Cole, Lampard to continue his impressive [even unlikely] improvement and Rooney [possibly even Joe Cole] to develop through to the championships).

A Quiz of Two Halves

First Half

(1) Who is the greatest number 7 recently to represent England?

(2) Which game drew the biggest crowd and smallest crowd of the following European Championship qualifiers? England 2-0 Turkey, England 2-0 Liechtenstein, Turkey 0-0 England?

(3) Who scored more goals in European qualifying for Portugal 2004, David Beckham or Michael Owen?

(4) Who scored the penalties and how many were there?

(5) Apart from Brazil in the World Cup England have lost few games in recent times. However one such defeat was 3-1 to Australia. Despite fielding Jeffers and Konchesky amongst 11 half-time substitutes do the Aussies nonetheless believe they are better than us?

Answers

5: Yes, but the Ashes will be ours, oh yes, they will

And of course there was the one that was spectacularly missed...

Istanbul   3: They both scored five   4: Beckham got two penalties and Owen one.

48,000 at the Stadium of Light for Turkey and the 42,000 packed into Fenerbahçe stadium in

2: More than 64,000 saw England struggle past Liechtenstein at old Trafford. More than the

1: David Beckham, but only because they gave the number 10 shirt to Matt Le Tiss

Second Half

6 Where you come from, do they put the kettle on?

7 What must you do whether fast or slow?

8 Despite all the years of hurt, what have we never stopped doing?

9 They'll be thinking of us where?

10 What are we going to find a way to do?

Answers

6: La la la la, and we're all like vindaloo, we're gonna score one more than you, Eng-land!
7: Get to the line 8: Dreaming 9: Back home 10: A way to get away, doing it all together, we'll do it right

Back from the Brink: Bulgaria

Seems like an eternity ago. You remember don't you,
1994...that baldy bloke and Bulgaria beating the Germans?
Well after that Euro 1996 was a bit of a disappointment and
Bulgaria were in danger of slipping off the footballing map
and becoming more famous for cut-price resorts on the
Black Sea which you really should get to before they're
spoiled – so they say. But now, here they are...finishing
ahead of Belgium and Croatia in Group 8, with both those
teams ranked in the world top 20 while Bulgaria languish –
barely inside the top 40 at 39.

And all this seems to be down to none other than
Plamen Markov. Who? Precisely! And that's what they were
saying in Bulgaria about a man whose successful (though
not outstanding) international playing career was mostly
followed by managing Bulgarian second division teams with
household names like Chardafon Gabrovo, FC Minion and
Vidima-Rakovski – household names at least if you lived in
any of those places.

But despite initial measured criticism which one might
loosely translate as 'what the f***ing hell did we choose this
Markov loser for?', 'Pla', as he is possibly known to his
friends, has organised the best of the old with up and
coming youngsters into something resembling a football
team. Players such as Dimitar Berbatov of Bayer
Leverkusen and Georgi Peev of Dinamo Kiev give them half
a chance combined with up and coming youngsters from
Levski and CSKA of Sofia. Predicted to be the big
disappointment of Euro 2004, however, will be Svetoslav

Todorov – any player good enough for Pompey isn't good enough for me.

Rumour has it that Markov is a little disappointed about the international retirement of Krassimir Balakov at age 37. As to the footballing merits of the individual I really couldn't care less, but along with Seaman it is another potential comedy commentary moment gone. Let's just hope that Paraguay's Chiqui Arce is still playing in Germany 2006.

Prediction

Having disappointed in Euro 96 and not arrived at Euro 2000 Bulgaria will be keen to do better this time around. However the missing sweet left-foot of Balakov and the early retirement (age 28) of Charlton's Radostin Kishishev in order to concentrate on his club commitments may leave the Bulgarians a little short, especially in defence. Though they have plenty of attacking options it is doubtful they have the necessary guile to break down the toughest defences whilst at the same time having potential vulnerabilities at the back.

Eliminated at the group stage.

A Quiz of Two Halves

First Half

1. How many goals did Dimitar Bebatov score in qualifying from Group 8?

2. Why did Belgium care more about Bulgaria's one defeat in Group 8 than Bulgaria?

3. How many Bulgarian players of recent times have names which do not end in the letter 'v'?

4. True or false? In recent times, Bulgarian home friendlies have attracted crowds below 10,000 whilst their European Championship qualifiers have averaged over 40,000.

5. Oh, it's really bugging me, what was the name of that bald bloke from 1994?

Answers

1: Five   2: It came in Bulgaria's last game; Bulgaria had already qualified and it allowed Croatia to make the play-off's instead of Belgium on the basis of the record between the two teams   3: Just the three, Pazin, Zagorcic and Jankovic   4: True. 21 August 2002 and 10,000 watch a friendly draw against Germany whilst two games later 42,000 watch tiny Andorra pour forwards for an equaliser as Bulgaria hold on to a 2-1 victory and three priceless points   5: Please write to Lloyd Pettiford, c/o The Department of International Studies, The Nottingham Trent University, Nottingham.

146

Second Half

6 Great Uncle Bulgaria is the mascot of AFC Wimbledon (i.e. the real Wimbledon with real supporters). False or false?

7 Who were Bulgarian Champions in 2002/03?

8 Who won the cup in 2002/03?

9 Rilski Sportist were one of two relegated teams. How many games did they win?

10 How many teams were promoted for the 2003/04 season?

Answers

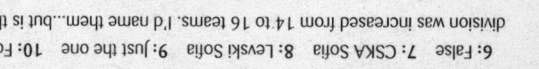

6: False 7: CSKA Sofia 8: Levski Sofia 9: Just the one 10: Four, because the top division was increased from 14 to 16 teams...but I'd name them, but is there really any point?

Bloody Hell, How Did They Get Here?: Greece

Who can forget Greece's performance in the World Cup in 1994? Well me, for one, and I suspect most of Greece too. I seem to remember the US Greeks getting very 'whoopy' – as Americans tend to – and excited, but that's about it. They played Nigeria, perhaps somebody Eastern European and lost two games 4-0 and ended up with a playing record of played 3, lost 3, for 0, against 10. And now, 10 years later on they are ranked 26 in the world? That's 13 above Bulgaria! And them, and their bald bloke, I do remember from 10 years ago. Have Greece ever qualified for a major tournament since? I don't think so, and if they did it was even less memorable than 1994.

At this point I should say that some of my friends are Greek and I know that when they're not ordering women around they are a fiercely proud people. Because of that I don't want my message to be misunderstood. I have nothing against Greeks (very nice of the George Clooney look-a-like to watch Beckham's free-kick fly in) and find their country and its cheese pies (but not Retsina – ugh!) delightful. But let's get one thing absolutely clear your football team is absolutely bloody rubbish.

Greece's qualification was, indeed is, remarkable. Much of the story is outlined elsewhere in this book. But rather than look at that story again, let us instead look at goals scored by group winners as a league table.

1. France 29
2. Czech Republic 23
3. Sweden 19
4. Italy 17
5. Denmark 15
6. Switzerland 15
7. England 14
8. Bulgaria 13
9. Germany 13
10. Greece 8

Eight! And of all those teams, only Denmark (9) and Switzerland (11) had a significantly worse defensive record. Only Switzerland's +4 goal difference was the same as Greece's. In Greece's defence (did they do anything else?), Norway only scored nine and Latvia 10 in reaching the play-offs and Bosnia-Herzegovina made seven goals go a long way but...

But...even Scotland got 12! This was a group with three teams ranked outside FIFA's world top 50. A group with Northern Ireland and Armenia, and Greece managed to win it with eight goals. Apart from the 2-0 thrashings of Armenia and Northern Ireland Greece just kept beating people 1-0, after losing their first two games 2-0. And so, their record of six qualifying wins and 18 points, is bettered only by France (eight, 24 points), Czech Republic (seven, 22 points) and England (six, 20 points). So credit where credit's due but...

But...around 70% of qualifying teams scored more goals...including Cyprus, including Macedonia and including bloody Albania! Since I am about to explode with indignant disbelief, I suppose we should recognise that these were Euro qualifiers and Greece had a 'job to do'...and all credit to them, they did it averaging a goal a game. So what did their friendly results look like during that time?

Romania 0-1 Greece

Greece 0-0 Republic of Ireland

Cyprus 1-2 Greece

Greece 1-0 Norway

Austria 2-2 Greece

Greece 2-2 Slovakia

Hmmm...the Cyprus goal-fest is a bit misleading as the Greeks were 1-0 down to a penalty awarded by the (presumably Greek) Cypriot ref. But it is quite clear that Greece's tournament goal average is increased to a whopping 1.3 in friendlies, although playing the sparkling Irish and Norwegians is never going to help such averages.

So who are the players to produce such results. Household names? Well no, with the vast majority coming from Panathinaikos, Olympiakos and AEK Athens with the odd smattering from elsewhere, including Iraklis and PAOK Salonika, as well as Werder Bremen and Hanover in Germany, Roma and Perugia in Italy and – of course – Dimitrios Papadopoulos who, as well as winning the

stereotype name award – and at the time of writing just one cap – plies his trade at Burnley (which is possibly the only mention they get in this book). Oh and there's some guy called Dabizas newly-arrived at Leicester too and Stelios 'incredibly long other name won't fit on his shirt' at Bolton.

Prediction

How can I put this without using the words 'crap' 'Greece' and 'are' in a different order? How about this way…I look into my crystal ball. Ah yes it's clearing. There's much optimism in Athens. Bars have people crowding around television screens. Expectantly. I see a snowball. Yes it's definitely a snowball. Oh, it's travelling away from me. Where's it going? Oh, I can see a sign. It says 'Welcome to my home' and there's a figure next to it. He has a tail and horns and is dressed in red. The snowball passes him and into the house. Good luck, I shout.

Eliminated at the group stage.

A Quiz of Two Halves

First Half

1. True or false? Watching the Greek goalie who looks a lot like George Clooney on player-cam would be more entertaining than watching the real George Clooney in the film Solaris?

2. Do Greece's home crowds average over 10,000?

3. Beware of Greeks bearing gifts. True or false?

4. Who is Greece's top scorer from qualifying?

5. For whom does the Greek goal machine mentioned above currently turn out?

Answers

5: The best team in Germany, Werder Bremen

4: Haristeas has tucked away three including two in one game against Northern Ireland

3: Probably true. Gift-bearing Greeks *must* be more dangerous than ones in front of goal

2: Just, but only because 15,500 glory hunters turned out to see the spell-binding 1-0 qualification clinching game against Northern Ireland. Was never scoring goals part of the Good Friday agreement?

1: True. I mean have you ever seen that complete drivel?

Second Half

6 What is Stelios of Bolton's real name that won't fit on shirts, with a bonus point for the correct spelling?

7 Who did Stelios play for in 2002/03?

8 How many goals did he score and where did his team finish?

9 Arch rivals to the team mentioned in questions 7 and 8 were runners-up. Who were they and what was the winning margin?

10 In 2002/03 bottom club Giannina got how many points?

Answers

6: Giannakopoulos 7: Olympiakos 8: He was second top scorer with 15 goals and his team – Olympiakos – were champions 9: Panathinaikos were second to Olympiakos on goal difference 10: Despite winning six and drawing seven – which would have been enough to finish bottom third and go into a play-off with the third placed second division team – they were deducted 90 points for non-payment of players and thus finished on minus 65. Ionikos were thus reprieved and won the relegation/promotion play-off against Kalamaria 2-1. The great escape

Every Now and Again, We Make It: Switzerland

Ranked 43 in the world and only occasionally troubling the big boys of world soccer, it is perhaps surprising to see Switzerland having qualified for Portugal 2004. Part of the surprise for me is that they even bother to enter the tournament at all. After all, Britain and Denmark might be quite 'euro-sceptic' but neither can match the fanatical neutralism of Switzerland who aren't even properly in the United Nations such is their determination to remain aloof. Possibly they regard themselves as just too different to join in – certainly cuckoo clocks are weird – but actually this has precious little to do with football.

Part of the Swiss success might be that they have not experimented too much in recent times. No wholesale half-time substitutions here! Of course this might be a deliberate strategy to try and develop a settled side following recent disappointments, or else it might be that they just haven't got a great many talented players. Apart from Stephanie Henchoz name me a current Swiss international player? I think there's your answer...? (Possibly those you might have named, if you did, would be the heavily capped Chapuisat [who!] and and the European player most likely to rival Paraguay's Chiqui Arce for a name that sounds most like some kind of bottom – West Brom's Bernt Haas).

Anyway, the point is that Switzerland were able to top a tricky – if not actually intimidating – looking group, managing to finish ahead of Russia (condemned to a trip to Wales), Eire, Albania and Georgia. The secret of their success came with their home form, where they won three of the four games they won, including the crucial 2-0 victory over the Irish Republic. Away they managed only one win, against Eire – which turned out to be crucial – drawing with both Albania and Georgia.

Prediction

Well, if they get a game against Greece then I wouldn't bet against them winning a game, and really they are capable of causing a surprise. However, I recommend that you do not back the Swiss even though I have resisted the temptation to do lots of gags about their defence and cheese with holes in it.

Eliminated at group stage.

A Quiz of Two Halves

First Half

1 Switzerland's only defeat in qualifying came away to Russia. What was the score?

2 What was the highest crowd Switzerland played in front of in getting to the final?

3 Who was Switzerland's top scorer in qualifying?

4 Who is the most capped player in the Swiss team?

5 In which country other than Switzerland do many Swiss national team players earn a living?

Answers

1: Russia won 4-1 although the Swiss took the lead 2: 40,000 in their crucial win in Dublin 3: Frei got five 4: Stephane Chapuisat who – if he keeps getting picked – will hope to pick up a 100th cap sometime around the time of the finals 5: Germany with players at Hamburg, 1860 Munich, Werder Bremen, Freiburg and Borussia Monchengladbach

Second Half

6 Despite being land-locked, 'In the Navy' is still the most commonly played tune in Swiss discos to this day. True or false?

7 How many teams are there in the Swiss top division? Is it 10, 12, 18, or 20?

8 Who were Champions in 2002/03?

9 The 2002/03 cup final was between second-placed Basle and third-placed Neuchatel Xamax. What was the score?

10 This question has been deleted in original form for legal reasons. Instead we offer you this cut and paste comedy opportunity. Michael Jackson is a pop-star. The fourth placed Swiss team in 2002/03 were called Young Boys. Can you make a joke from any of this?

Answers

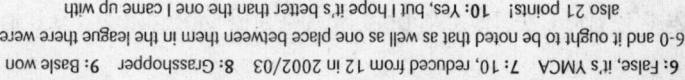

6: False, it's YMCA   7: 10, reduced from 12 in 2002/03   8: Grasshopper   9: Basle won 6-0 and it ought to be noted that as well as one place between them in the league there were also 21 points!   10: Yes, but I hope it's better than the one I came up with

Almost as Difficult to Write Off as the Germans: Czech Republic

The Czechs won the European Championships in 1976, although in those days with the help of their friends and neighbours the Slovaks. In the final they beat the Germans on penalties. That is a fact I suspect I have mentioned elsewhere in the book and which I would be tempted to repeat several times, except the editors have got a bit wise to that 'joke' and threatened not to pay me if I keep wasting words by repeating all things anti-German. In any case, 20 years later when Germany had absorbed the former East Germany and the Czechs had agreed an amicable separation with the Slovaks, the Germans extracted revenge with a dodgy 2-1 win 'golden goal' final victory.

Despite such facts, and a reasonable record in the World Cup (two finals, although in 1934 and 1962) the Czech Republic still seem to be regarded as dark horses in world soccer despite ranking 11 in the current FIFA rankings. This time is probably no different with few people talking of them as serious contenders. In fact, so under-rated are they that when I was writing the French section of this book, there I was writing 'France fantastic blah, great record, blah blah' that I actually transposed the score for France v Czech Republic. The French were not unbeaten. They lost 2-0 at home to the Czechs in February 2003. The Czechs also beat Serbia and Montenegro 5-0 in a friendly (the same team which held Italy and beat Wales twice each in qualifying) and Turkey 4-0.

The Czechs' qualifying record has been absolutely spectacular and second only to France. The only points dropped were away to Holland, where they recovered from a goal down to take a point. Additionally, and unlike France, they really haven't lost for a long time, trouncing opponents at will. Only the Dutch, and the Swedes in a 3-3 friendly have escaped undefeated. Given that they failed to qualify for the last World Cup – losing disappointingly in a play-off against Belgium – this form is all the more remarkable.

The odd thing is that whilst you might expect the 7-foot 8-inch tall Koller to knock in a few goals and Nedved to provide quality in midfield, you probably don't expect Vladimir Smicer (Vlad the Incapable), Milan Baros and Karel Poborsky to knock them in too. But that's what has happened as goals have come from all round the park; although admittedly most of Smicer's have come in friendlies, proving that he really is a small game player. In the qualifiers themselves, Koller scored six. Also on the score sheet were Nedved (2), Baros (3), Smicer (2), Jankulovski (3), Poborsky (2), Rosicky (1), Lokvenc (2), Stajner (1) and Vachousek (1). Ten outfield players getting on the score sheet in qualifying is very healthy indeed, and during the same period several others also managed goals in friendlies.

So, being able to score from anywhere and undefeated under their current coach (Karel Bruckner) the Czechs are in confident mood. The coach's appointment was interesting and controversial, Bruckner having been assistant to the previous incumbent Jozef Chovanec who led the disastrous 2002 World Cup campaign and who had taken to personally criticising players. But although some players considered quitting the national team because of Bruckner's appointment (and Patrik Berger actually did; once again showing the exceptional judgement which took him to Fratton Park!) most stayed on and have been pleasantly surprised as morale has improved and as the new coach has successfully integrated players from the 2002 European Under-21 Championship winning team, including the inspirational performances of young Petr Cech in goal.

Prediction

When they make the finals, they usually don't muck about. The authority with which they beat Costa Rica 4-1 in 1990 for instance was most impressive, managing four times what the Scots failed to do at all. [Editor's note: Absolutely gratuitous mention of that game again; we can only apologise and offer a full refund to anyone who can convince us that Scottish domestic football is exciting]. But anyway, expect competence and perhaps the odd surprise; if Alexander Dubcek had hoped that Czechoslovakia could promote 'socialism with a human face' then the Czech football team very much represent the same grit, determination and efficiency that we have come to expect from the Germans, except that we quite like them.[16]

Quarter-finals but probably no farther.

[16] All of this applies only unless they play England, in which case delete all the niceness.

A Quiz of Two Halves

First Half

1. From August 2002 until the end of qualifying the Czechs averaged more than three goals per game. True or false?

2. What did they average in qualifying?

3. Such is the Czech-Slovak rivalry that a friendly match between the teams in August 2002 had a recorded attendance 11,985 above the official safety limit, leading to a European fine and closure of the Dubcek Stadium in Prague. True or false?

4. Roughly what percentage of current Czech capped players play their domestic football in the Republic?

5. Which Prague team provides the most players for the national team?

Answers

1: True, 41 goals in 13 matches   2: Just under three at 23 goals in eight matches
3: False, unless the Dubcek Stadium really exists and has a capacity of one. In fact 11,986 turned up in total in Olomouc to see the Czechs recover from a goal down to win 4-1
4: About 50%   5: It's probably 50/50 between Slavia and Sparta Prague

Second Half

6 How many of the Czech goalkeepers and defenders at Euro 2004 are likely to have over 30 caps?

7 Which team sharing a name with the Irish League champions for 2002/03 were relegated in that year?

8 Which team from the town which gave its name to beer got promoted for the 2003/04 season?

9 Which player who impressed at Euro 96, only to flop thereafter, was Czech player of the season in 2002/03? Clue: he has a girl's name and hair

10 How many people watched the Czech Cup final between Jablonec and Teplice (won by the latter 1-0). Was it 5,833 – 13,402 – 29,003 – 50,000 or 67,774.

Answers

6: None. At the time of writing Marek Jankulovski has the most caps from this group with 22
7: Bohemians   8: Viktoria Plzen (Pilsner)   9: Karel Poborsky   10: Just 5,833

Could You Be More Surprised?: Latvia

In *World Soccer Yearbook 2003* all the other qualifying teams are set out nicely, with photos, a whole page each (including record of appearances etc) and helpful formatting. The Latvians meanwhile are squeezed unceremoniously between Kazakhstan and Liechtenstein, with the information crammed unhelpfully together, safe in the knowledge that no one will ever want it.

A look at their results from recent times (excluding the impressiveness against Turkey) fails to excite. The season opens with a 0-0 draw against Azerbaijan and 4-2 defeat by Belarus. Both those teams managed one win in qualification. Belarus scored as many in Riga as they did in the whole qualifying tournament. Despite this, the qualifiers themselves begin with a 0-0 draw against table-topping Sweden. Latvia are the only team to prevent Sweden scoring in qualifying, a feat they perform once again in Stockholm to ensure qualification. In fact the four points Latvia take from Sweden, compared to the nil points that Poland manage turn out to be crucial.

But after that first 0-0 draw no one would really have expected the Latvians to progress. Even after a 1-0 win in Poland, the same result in San Marino hardly gave the impression that they were likely to keep going, any more than you would have thought Wales would. And indeed the bubble did seem to burst. After winning 3-0 at home to San Marino and taking the lead in Hungary, they then lost that game 3-1. When that loss was followed up by defeat at home to Poland (the 2-0 score-line giving the Poles aggregate advantage in any head-to-head points situation) it looked like the game was up.

A narrow home win against Hungary at least gave the Latvians a chance, but it still looked like they would need to get something in Sweden. And though they managed that, no one then really expected them to beat Turkey, certainly not when trailing with 25 minutes to go in Istanbul! And all of this without the Latvian Michael Owen, Marian Pahars!

So who have they got then? Well you've possibly heard of Alex Kolinko? (Bench-warming goalie at Crystal Palace). Or Igor Stepanovs? (Bench-warming defender at Arsenal). OK, Imants Bleidelis? (Erstwhile bench-warmer at Southampton, from whence he came at half time in the FA Cup tie v Tranmere which Saints led 3-0 after 45 minutes and then lost 4-3). Well all of these players seem to have performed better for country than club, the only exception perhaps to this rule being Pahars when fit. And one player you may now have heard of after the winner in Riga and equaliser in Istanbul is Maris Verpakovskis.

Prediction

Commentators everywhere, having practised those awkward Turkish names in 2002, are now cursing the qualification of Messers Blagonadezdins, Zakresevskis, Kolesnicenko and Prohorenkovs. If Pahars is fit again, maybe just maybe him and Verpakovskis can do the damage to take them even further. That would have to be an outside chance, but Latvia got a win and a draw against Turkey in two games and by my book that's impressive whether it's England or Latvia.

Eliminated at group stage.

A Quiz of Two Halves

First Half

1. With a goal in roughly every four games, who is currently Latvia's top scorer in internationals?

2. Marian Pahars played for Skonto Riga before moving to Southampton. But can you name any other Latvian teams?

3. Latvia won three of their four away games in qualifying. Which was their easiest and which most difficult win?

4. What does a Latvian flag look like?

5. In the play-off versus Turkey, Verpakovskis emerged as the goal-scoring hero, but in the qualifiers who scored the most out of Latvia's 10?

Answers

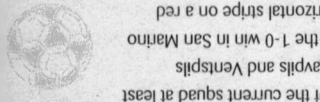

1: Marian Pahars with 15 goals in 56 matches   **2:** Thought not. Of the current squad at least one comes from each of Metalurgs Liepaja, Dinaburg Daugavpils and Ventspils   **3:** Technically the 2-0 win in Poland was most comfortable, while the 1-0 win in San Marino came courtesy only of a last-minute own goal   **4:** A white horizontal stripe on a red background   **5:** It was Verpakovskis again with four, although Bleidelis scored three

Second Half

6 True or false? This is the first major footballing tournament that not only Latvia but any of the former Soviet Baltic republics have qualified for?

7 Skonto Riga are like the Manchester United of Latvian football. However, the equivalents of Southampton, Charlton and Everton have some really strange names like: HB, KI, GI, B36, B68 and VB. True or false?

8 How many teams compete in the Latvian top division? Is it 20, 15, 10 or eight?

9 Why did bottom team Auda not get relegated for the 2003 season?

10 The 2002 cup final saw Skonto Riga thump Metalurgs 3-0 to complete the double. How many of their supporters turned up to see them to their triumph?

Answers

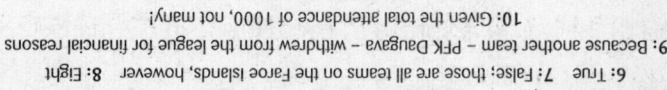

10: Given the total attendance of 1000, not many!

9: Because another team – PFK Daugava – withdrew from the league for financial reasons

6: True   7: False; those are all teams on the Faroe Islands, however   8: Eight

Against Slightly Unfavourable Odds: Croatia

After their first leg home draw against Slovenia, Croatia must have been ever such slight underdogs in the second leg despite their loftier world ranking. They become even more under-doggier after having Juventus' Igor Tudor sent off. However, they won through to qualify for another major tournament in their relatively brief post-Yugoslav existence, which reached a peak in the 1998 World Cup quarter-final when they beat Germany 3-0, *beat Germany 3-0*, only to lose to 10-man France in the semis. However, and despite the win against Germany, they had largely lost popular support by that stage – France's 10 man-ness being due to some appalling and blatant play-acting by Slaven Bilic.

It has to be said that the Croatia of today do not look capable of beating anyone 3-0. They look dour and dogged and if it wasn't for the recent emergence of the young Dado Prso scoring in both legs of the play-offs it is difficult to imagine they would have overcome Slovenia. Fortunately, an away goal to the good, the Slovenians decided to be even more dour and had no answer once Prso had scored. In 30 minutes against 10 men they barely managed a shot.

Many of the Croatian team play for the relatively well known domestic teams of Hadjuk Split and Dinamo Zagreb as well as the slightly less well known Varteks Varazdin. The rest of the squad is spread all over Europe in Germany,

Greece, Italy, Austria, Belgium, France and England as well as *outside* Europe in Israel in the case of Giovanni Rosso. Despite unhappiness with the coach and the team not being what it once was, Croatia still have a decent team. In recent friendlies they drew 2-2 with Macedonia (having trailed twice) and beat Sweden which makes them at least as good as England, wouldn't you say?

Prediction

Croatia no longer hold any surprises and – Prso notwithstanding – in the post Boksic and Suker days they appear to offer very little indeed. The shirts may still attract a certain novel charm but that's about all.

Eliminated at group stage.

A Quiz of Two Halves

First Half

(1) Dado Prso, play-off hero scoring both Croatia's goals, managed how many in qualifying?

(2) Who scored most goals for Croatia in qualifying?

(3) True or false? Dado Prso has the shortest name in the Croatian team?

(4) Assuming Boksic not to be a part of the current Croatian squad, how many have got into double figures?

(5) Which current Croatian player has scored the most goals?

Answers

1: Just the one. Against Belgium   2: Nico Kovac and Milan Rapajic both netted twice
3: True and false. Leko, Olic, Srna, Agic and Bule all have only four letters in their second
name. Only Nino Bule however can match the eight letter total and no one
is able to beat it   4: One   5: Goran Vlaovic

Second Half

6 How many has the player in Question 5 scored and was this at a faster or slower rate than Latvia's Marian Pahars?

7 Who won the Croatian league in 2002/03?

8 The champion's and league's top scorer was Ivica Olic with 16. Who second top scored at Dinamo and in the league as a whole?

9 But he was rubbish at Villa or somewhere wasn't he?

10 What were the results in the 2003 cup final?

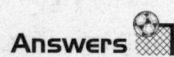

Answers

6: 15 in fewer games than a similar number for the pacey Saints striker: **7:** Dinamo **8:** Bosko Balaban **9:** Yes, I believe that to be the case **10:** First leg – Uljanik 0 Hadjuk Split 1. Second leg – Hadjuk Split 4 Uljanik 0, although since Uljanik are not in the top division, I guess that's not bad?

Unlikely to Impress in the Finals: Spain

Apart from losing at home to Greece, Spain qualified relatively easily. True a 0-0 draw in Belfast forced them into a play-off, true they trailed 1-0 at home and only just escaped with a win, but ultimately they cruised past a rather disappointing Norwegian side. However, and such was the case also in qualifying for Japan/Korea, cruising through qualifiers has never so much been Spain's problem as much as actually producing it on the big stage.

Spain are allegedly now ranked third in the world, but rather like recently inflated rankings for Colombia or the USA, no one will be particularly quaking. Unlike those other teams of course, Spain really do have enough talent that other teams ought to be quaking. In a pattern the reverse of France all of these talented players are currently playing in Spain with club representation at the time of writing roughly as follows:

1. Real Madrid (7)
2. Barcelona (4)
3. Deportivo La Coruna (5)
4. Betis (3)
5. Celta Vigo (1)
6. Athletic Bilbao (2)
7. Atletico Madrid (2)
8. Valencia (5)

9.   Valladolid (1)
10.   Real Sociedad (3)
11.   Malaga (1)
12.   Espanyol (1)

Raul Bravo's temporary spell at Leeds in 2002/03 is the
exception which proves this rule. The big question is
whether all the great players we are talking about can
produce the goods in Portugal. The answer, as always, is
almost certainly 'no' as we watch talented individuals freeze
on the big stage. Is it the political structure of Spain such
that the different nationalities (Basque, Catalan etc) do not
feel really Spanish? Actually who cares as long as they
don't suddenly sort it out if they should face England)

Prediction

Unlikely to have the support of many Portuguese neutrals,
but should get through the group stage. Despite their world
ranking, Spain hardly look like world beaters when it
matters and time and time again they have proved they are
not!

Get through group stage. Won't get to final.

A Quiz of Two Halves

First Half

(1) Despite Wales' impressive average crowd during qualification, Spain played in front of the largest crowd in qualification. Against which team?

(2) How many goals did Raul score in the qualifiers at group stage?

(3) Ruben Baraja scored twice against Northern Ireland. What other important goal did he score in qualification?

(4) Spain scored 16 goals in qualifying. How many were scored in the first half?

(5) Of the four goals Spain conceded in qualifying how many were in the first half?

Answers

4: Just three 5: Two

1: Ukraine, 82,000 2: Five 3: The winner at home to Norway in the play-offs

Second Half

(6) How did Spain lose at home to Greece in qualifying?

(7) How many Real teams are there in the Spanish Primera Liga in 2003/04?

(8) Who top scored in Spain in 2002/03?

(9) Which tiny team who had looked rooted to the foot of the table almost escaped relegation (but didn't) and lost in the Spanish Cup final?

(10) Of the top six scorers in the Primera Liga for 2002/03 only one was Spanish. Who?

Answers

6: Nobody really knows   **7:** OK, I'm doing this off the top of my head, so apologies if I got it wrong but I think this is the list...Real Madrid, Real Sociedad, Real Betis, Real Osasuna, Real Mallorca, Real Murcia and Real Zaragoza. That makes seven. But if you're gonna be a clever clogs you should also add Villarreal!   **8:** Despite his efforts for the Dutch national team, it was Roy Maakay – then of Deportivo La Coruna – with 29   **9:** Poor old Recreativo Huelva   **10:** Raul, behind a Dutchman (Maakaay), a Turk (Nihat), a Brazilian (Ronaldo), a Serb (Kovacevic) and tied with another Dutchman (Kluivert)

It'll Just Cause More Arguments: Holland

Being edged out by the Czechs and then losing in Glasgow probably pushed the Dutch closer to elimination than they would have hoped. All of this in turn probably caused more arguments, possibly when someone on the bench in Glasgow started sniggering when the crowd started singing 'he's bald, he's fat, he's gonna get the sack, Advocaat.' The Dutch are great at arguments. Given the talent they have – Holland B would have beaten Scotland in a play-off – one wonders what they might achieve if they stopped trying to be more arrogant than the Germans[17] and started pulling together. After missing out on Japan/Korea, failure to beat the Scots and qualify this time would probably have meant a third world war in the Dutch camp.

No one has ever really worked it out but the Dutch just don't seem to be able to play nicely together. Thus the list of talent is amazing from back to front: Van der Sar, De Boer, Cocu, Zenden, Overmars...all hugely talented, with the possible exception of Boudewijn. And the strikers! OK, so most of them have personality 'issues' but what a selection! Patrick Kluivert has been the most successful at international level, but then they've got some bloke called Van Nistelrooy, Roy Makaay, Jimmy Floyd Hasselbaink *and* Pierre Van Hooijdonkey! Wow! The trouble is Patrick

[17] As football genius Berti Vogts pointed out, German 'arrogance' is German 'confidence' and in their case is usually directed towards a team effort.

doesn't like Ruud and Jimmy doesn't like anyone. Rumour has it that Pierre stole Roy's comb and Pierre will only play with Patrick if it's a midweek fixture. Hey, who knows what's going on?

Unlucky to have to go through the play-offs thanks to coming up against the resurgent Czechs, Holland then did well to win against Scotland despite Vogts' team putting up a spirited display in the first leg of the play-offs. In friendlies over the past year Holland have drawn with 2004 hosts Portugal and thrashed Germany 3-1 away with Kluivert, Hasselbaink and Van Nistelrooy all getting on the score sheet. The Dutch actually seem to get more pleasure out of beating the Germans than we do! If they can just get along like good children now...

Prediction

Having got there Holland are unlikely to be a big flop, but similarly unlikely to really go all the way. That said, the European Championships are possibly more their thing than World Cups. Expect this vast array of talent to reach the quarter-finals even if the manager is sulking and none of the players are talking to each other. Don't be surprised if they reach the semis. But don't bank on them getting any further.

Get through group stage. Won't get to final.

A Quiz of Two Halves

First Half

1 How many Dutch players have scored 10 or more goals for the national team

2 The seven above does not include Jimmy Floyd Hasselbaink. True or false?

3 Which player, despite being prolific in domestic football, averages less than a goal per 10 games for Holland?

4 Who has the strangest first name in the Dutch team?

5 Why does Edgar Davids wear those funny things like glasses when playing?

Answers

5: It's related to the condition glaucoma but I'll not kid you I know all the details

4: Edwin, Jaap, Wilfred, Edgar, Clarence, Wesley or Arjen – probably

1: seven   2: True, although he is on nine at the time of writing   3: Roy Makaay

Second Half

(6) While England was losing to Australia at football in February (who cares after the Rugby!) who were Holland playing and beating?

(7) How many points separated the top three clubs in the Dutch top division in 2002/03?

(8) What were the names of the clubs in question 7?

(9) How many points separated third placed Feyernoord from fourth placed NAC?

(10) The Dutch Cup final of 2003 was between Utrecht (47 points in the league) and Feyernoord. Was the score 2-0 to Feyernoord, 6-0 to Feyernoord or 4-1 to Utrecht?

Answers

10: 4-1 to Utrecht

7: four   8: Unsurprisingly PSV 84 points, Ajax 83 and Feyernoord 80   9: A mere 28

6: Argentina through a Van Bronckhorst goal in the last five minutes

Russia

I may have added something subsequently, but it may be significant that I couldn't really think of any headline to attach to Russia. Despite scoring a few at home, they qualified unspectacularly behind Switzerland thanks largely to an unexpected defeat in Georgia. In beating Wales 1-0 over two legs in a play-off they then showed themselves to be technically efficient but boring enough to bore even the staunchest football fan. But going back to even the 'great' Soviet sides efficiency has always won out over style.

In fact, the story of Russia's qualification is most odd. Two home victories with four goals each were followed up with two away defeats to table proppers Albania (3-1) and Georgia (1-0). At this point Russia must have feared the worst, but fighting come-from-behind draws away to Switzerland (2-0 to 2-2) and Ireland (1-1) put them back in with a chance. At that point they scored three and four in winning their final two home games, prior to the efficient elimination of Wales.

Famous names in the Russian team are few and far between, with the most famous players from that part of the world tending to be Ukrainian these days. Some will have heard of Beschastnykh even if they have trouble spelling it. Alexei Smertin may also have come to the attention of some readers following a misguided move to Portsmouth.

Prediction

Tidy uninspiring football will only get you so far at international level, and in Russia's case it has probably already taken them as far as it will. They might possibly sneak through the group stage (though only as runners-up) but I wouldn't bet a great deal on such an outcome.

Eliminated at group stage

A Quiz of Two Halves

First Half

1 Several of the Russian squad play for a team named after a planet. Which one?

2 Who does Denis Laktionov play for?

3 Which team provides most players for the Russian squad?

4 Which other teams from Moscow also contribute players to the national team?

5 Name some other teams in Russia.

Answers

1: Saturn   2: Suwon Bluewings in South Korea   3: CSKA Moscow
4: At least Spartak, Lokomotiv, Dinamo and Torpedo   5: Zenit St Petersburg, Rotor Volgograd, Krylya Sovetov and Saturn of course

Second Half

(6) What we need is a strong leader like Stalin to sort us out?

(7) Lokomotiv Moscow and CSKA Moscow both finished the 2002 season on 66 points but the latter had a goal difference of +34 compared to the former's +32. Why did CSKA not win the championship?

(8) Who won the 2002/03 Russian Cup final?

(9) True or false? The Russian Cup winner's opponents Rostov had completed the previous championship under the name Rostselmash.

(10) Russia?

Answers

6: Vasily Yanaev, former defender of Stalingrad, now 92 and steadily sipping vodka in small unwelcoming bar in a Moscow suburb says 'yes'. **7:** Because it was settled by a play-off, which Lokomotiv won 1-0 **8:** Just to p*** CSKA off a bit more, that went to Spartak Moscow **9:** Not interesting, but true **10:** I never even met 'er.

Where to Go If This European Championship Guide Has Left You With a Thirst for Knowledge

If this hastily and randomly thrown together selection of facts leaves you yelling 'I must know more!', here's where to go – although you may need to learn a foreign language first of course...

Bulgaria: www.bfunion.bg

Croatia: www.hns-cff.hr

Czech Republic: www.fotbal.cz

Denmark: www.dbu.dk

England: www.TheFA.com

France: www.fff.fr

Germany: www.dfe.de

Greece: www.epo.gr

Holland: www.knvb.nl

Italy: www.figc.it

Latvia: www.lff.lv

Portugal: www.fpf.pt

Russia: www.rfs.ru

Spain: www.rfef.es

Sweden: www.svenskfotboll.se

Switzerland: www.football.ch

Chapter 4

The Key Players

Introduction

Many people would agree that Jimmy Greaves was the finest player of his generation. But when it came to England winning the World Cup of 1966 he was not the key player, Geoff Hurst was. Similarly, many people would agree that Matthew Le Tissier was the most talented player of his generation. Indeed what sane person could disagree? But when England cried out for a bit of creativity – or even a decent penalty taker – he was not there. A potentially key player, not even on the bench or part of the armoury. The point of this then is that the players selected below are not necessarily the team's best players (although many are included), but the players who will need to perform above their best, or to emerge this summer, if their particular nation is really to go far in the tournament. (Anyone tempted to take the occasional Pompey related jibe too seriously should note that I personally stand shoulder to shoulder with Portsmouth fans, but only in the face of a common enemy – i.e. Australian cricket – as part of the Barmy Army).

Bulgaria: Dimitar Berbatov and the Rest of the Team

Currently playing for Bayer Leverkusen in Germany with around 25 caps and an impressive goals per game ratio of above one goal every two games, Dimitar Berbatov is quick and moves well and is perhaps the stand-out player of the Bulgarians. But for them to shine it will need several players to emerge as big time players in the same tournament. As for instances, Georgi Peev of Dynamo Kiev, the much improved Stilian Petrov and the attacking left-sided midfielder Martin Petrov (no relation of Stilian). As for the defence it looks vulnerable and the coach has had to experiment; he will need to be something of an alchemist if he is to get the blend right for 2004. But if he does, it will be very much a team effort in support of Berbatov.

Among possible 'late runs' into stardom might be Georgi Chilikov. Scoring 22 goals for Levski Sofia in 2002/03 he thus topped the scoring charts by five goals from his nearest rival in a 26 game season. He has now broken into the national team, scoring the first in Bulgaria's unimpressive 2-1 home win over Andorra for instance. At 26 he will be at or around his peak for the tournament if he can dislodge some of the more established forwards permanently. More of a gamble in terms of likely impact – in fact probably about 10,000-1 against to score the winner in the final in Portugal – is Todorov. No not the bloke at Portsmouth – goodness me, he must be about 1,000,000-1 against...no I mean Anatoli Todorov, an under-21 international who helped his club side Lovech to the Bulgarian Cup final (where they lost to Chilikov's Levski).

Coach: Plamen Markov

A Very Quick Quiz

The goal and performance of which Bulgarian saw Germany eliminated from USA 94?
- a) Emil Kostadinov
- b) Krassimir Balakov
- c) Stilian Petrov
- d) Yucan Fukov
- e) Letchkov

Answers

e: Letchkov. I finally remembered it but I'm still not sure of the first name or the spelling!

187

Croatia: The Unpronounceables

By which I mean Dado Prso and Dario Srna. The strength of the Croatian side is undoubtedly going to be maximised if the old guard of Boksic and Suker can be effectively replaced by the younger generation. At the moment the signs of this are somewhat faltering but not altogether discouraging as a tricky play-off tie against Slovenia was negotiated with all the style, grace and tension which might be displayed by a debutant high-wire performer.

Dario Srna hasn't long been in the national team and will be just 22 at the time of the tournament. He earned his call-up after banging in a hat-trick for the Under-21s and went on to score the opener against Belgium (after nine minutes) in what turned out to be a decisive 4-0 qualifying victory, thus taking the Croats into the play-offs on head-to-head basis v Belgium, losing only 2-1 away. Not so much a goal-scorer, and more of a provider, Srna could be important in these championships and a worry for England.

Another young player who may yet emerge is Dinamo Zagreb's teenage star Niko Kranjcar, who captained his side to the Croatian championship at the age of 18 and despite being the youngest player in the division. We all know there are three paths ahead for the talented youngster. He will do one of the following: get his chance and take to it like a duck to water or get his chance and look hopelessly out of his depth or not get his chance thanks to overly conservative football management such that when he finally does it will be too late. That's what disgracefully happened to Matt Le Tiss, though not Owen and Rooney. In any case Niko has all the right attributes.

Oddly enough the real emerging talent for Croatia will be almost 30 by the time of the championships in Portugal. Dado Prso, also banging them in for Monaco – affording excellent limerick-writing opportunities as if that has anything to do with anything – was on the score-sheet (like Srna) in the crucial win against Belgium. Since then he scored both Croat goals in the 2-1 aggregate win against Slovenia in the play-offs. He is thus 'on the crest of a wave'; if he can ride it all the way to Portugal, he will need to score more crucial goals if Croatia are to do well.

Coach: Otto Baric

A Very Quick Quiz

Change only one word and then rearrange the following into a puerile limerick which doesn't quite scan:

a) There once was a man called Prso

b) For the size of his banana

c) Though he did get some stick

d) Sticking out wherever he'd go

e) Who played for his team Monaco

 **Answers**

The word to change is banana and the order is a, e, c, b and d. With apologies

Czech Republic: Petr Cech

Recently promoted from the all-conquering Czech Under-21 team, Petr Cech must be the finest young goal-keeper in Europe, notwithstanding the shot-stopping abilities of Iker Casillas of Real Madrid and Spain. At the time of writing Petr is turning out for Rennes in France, although he will surely attract interest from bigger clubs in the future. [STOP PRESS: Petr has just signed up for Roman's army at Chelsea next season, demonstrating – as if further demonstration were necessary – Lloyd's uncanny ability to predict the future – Ed.] His performances have instilled confidence throughout the Czech team and he is the only keeper – since the World Cup of course – to shut out the current European Champions France.

You might be tempted to suggest that if players such as Smicer and Poborsky can replicate the form they showed in the Premiership it's not going to matter how poor 'old' Petr plays! However, Smicer has always looked a different proposition in a Czech shirt – or was that a check shirt. Anyway, never mind Vlad the Ineffectual, it's the form of Poborsky that might be of more interest. Despite the disappointment of his stay at Manchester United he is now enjoying something of an Indian summer in the Czech Republic. He returned to Sparta Prague from Italy as the league's highest paid player and has proved all the doubting Tomases (that's the Czech spelling not a typo)

wrong. In his first season, Sparta regained the championship from arch-rivals Slavia by a single point.

Another 'golden oldie' is Pavel Nedved who had a fantastic season in 2002/03 for Juventus. Many feel that his team's Champions League final defeat to Milan was as a direct result of Nedved being suspended and Juventus missing his power, pace and finishing, which he seems to have moved up, rather than down, a gear as he moves into his 30s. One really confusing thing about Pavel is why Barry Davies – unless he speaks Czech of course – seems to want to extract the same ridiculous noises out of 'Nedved' as he previous reserved for Ole Gunnar 'Solskjaer'? It's like some kind of demented 'Neee-ed-vee-ed' noise. Still, unlikely to put the man off.

Apart from Petr Cech, the Czech's have plenty of young talent. 2002's Czech young player of the year – one of the doubting Tomases – Hubschman is a solid defender. His successor as young player of the year Vaclav Sverkos is a forward with unfashionable Banik Ostrava for whom he scored 14 goals (second highest in the league) in 2002/03. Whether he is still with them by the time you read this may have much to do with his chances of breaking into the Czech national team – such is the way of the world alas. But one potentially to watch.

Coach: Karel Bruckner

A Very Quick Quiz

Which is the correct pronounciation of Pavel Nedved's
surname according to Barry Davies?

a) Noose Vacuum
b) Nobble Vash
c) Neeee-ed-veee-ed
d) Nedved
e) Melon

Answers

Possibly all except d

Denmark:
Claus Jensen

Charlton favourite Claus may not be everyone's choice as a
key player, but in the absence of Stig Tofting's creative
genius, not to mention the Laudrups, midfield is where
Denmark are going to need excellent performances. Up
front they have reliable strikers in Rommedahl, Tomasson
and Sand but it is a player like Jensen – at the peak of his
career in his mid twenties – whom they really need to have
a special tournament. His record so far of five goals from a
little over 20 caps is fine, but he may just provide that bit
more and take the Danes further than people expect. You
might say ditto Gravesen (Everton, looks 38 but will be 28),
Jensen (Man City, 29) and Poulsen (Schalke 04, 24).

But perhaps it is also at the upper and lower range of
Denmark's midfield that we need to look for inspiration?
Someone you wouldn't really expect to be at the peak of
their career by summer 2004 is Morten Wieghorst. In fact
he will be 33. However, returning to Brondby from Celtic
he has overcome injury as well as illness and won back his
place in the Denmark team. It seems perhaps doubtful
however that he will be a major force at these
championships – although with Denmark you just never
know. Also in the Brondby midfield and tipped to be the
next Danish superstar is Thomas Kahlenberg. Given the
freedom to roam by none other than Michael Laudrup
(Brondby coach) Thomas (aged 21) has proved the

doubting Niclases wrong. Having just been promoted to the Danish national team, the time is right for him to emerge in Portugal.

Coach: Morten Olsen

A Very Quick Quiz

Which of the following footballers looks most like Denmark and Everton's Thomas Gravesen?

a) Uncle Fester
b) Paul Gascoigne
c) Peter Beardsley
d) Thomas Gravesen
e) Lee Carsley

Answers

e) Lee Carsley

England: Wayne Rooney

Much has been expected from 'Roonaldo' and so far he has done pretty well. Living up to your potential week in week out is difficult for anybody in any job but for Wayne in the national spotlight it must be even more so. If he can keep playing well enough to justify selection, the tournament itself may well be the spring-board to super mega stardom. With a strong core to the team already existing in the shape of Campbell, Beckham and Owen, the 'unknown' quantity of Rooney may well be the added ingredient that makes all the difference.

Another less spectacular Wayne is Bridge. Hopefully his move to Chelsea, as well as being bloody irritating, will also improve his international chances. With an even temperament and solid defensive qualities, as well as an ability to get forward, he has the potential to set the nerves jangling less often than Ashley Cole. Another nerve-jangler is David James. Since he appears to have emerged as Sven's choice ahead of Paul Robinson and others, we can only hope that 'Calamity' gets the errors out of his system and is either dropped before next summer, or continues to produce the form that allowed him two clean sheets against the Turks.

Coach: Sven Goran Eriksson

A Very Quick Quiz

When England win in Portugal, we will have achieved a unique feat of winning major championships in sports that matter in consecutive years. But can you remember what the score was when England won the Rugby World Cup of 2003 to do the first leg of this achievement?

a)   Australia lost so who cares

b)   England won so who cares

c)   What makes the Aussies (whinging Matildas) really sore is that they actually played their best and got some really dodgy refereeing decisions and still lost

d)   Australia 17-20 England

e)   Australia 17-20 Engerland (after extra time)

Answers

All of the above

France:
Big Zidane and
Little Zidane

Zinedine Zidane – a world-class player who played injured and consequently badly in the 2002 World Cup. At 32, Portugal 2004 may well be the last tournament at which he himself expects to be able to perform at or about his best. Many consider that France's failure in 2002 was mainly due to this man being unable to perform and he may well be the key to whether they turn things around this time. Zidane is the pivot around which all things attacking turn. Sylvain Wiltord looks a much better player for France than Arsenal and Thierry Henry and David Trezeguet (both averaging a little under a goal every two games but mainly because France score from everywhere!) thrive on the service Zidane provides.

With so many French players playing outside France and well known, it is to the French League itself – the imaginatively titled Ligue 1 – to which we must turn for potential surprise packages. Jerome Rothen of Monaco is one such player. He is a left-sided attacking midfielder who gets more than his fair share of assists. Now may just be the right time for getting into the French midfield. Despite the form of William Gallas, given the big sulk of Marcel Desailly, much the same might be said of the French back four with Lille's Eric Abidal pushing for a place too. In recent historical perspective, Lille having a player in the French team is akin to the likes of Birmingham, Charlton and Southampton having England internationals – only more so. Whatever, Abidal has impressed hugely in 2003/04 and has been favourably compared to Lilian Thuram, although rumours that he was to change his name to Erica so that they could both have girls' names were wildly exaggerated. It has been a remarkable turn-around for a player not long ago loaned to Lille from Monaco because no one wanted to buy him. Having declared his wish to leave Lille – ah such gratitude and loyalty – he may be playing for PSG (or a team near you) by the time you read this.

And, perhaps depressingly, France also have talent awaiting on the forward production line. Mourad Meghni – who will be 20 by the time of the tournament – is known as the 'Little Zidane' and not it must be said because he is balding in a more bizarre fashion than even Red Rum look-a-likey David Platt, but because he is incredibly skillful and has great vision. Eschewing France for Italy as a young boy he served an apprenticeship in the Bologna youth team before breaking into their first team and instantly being compared with former Bologna, Sampdoria and (did he really play for) Leicester (?) star Roberto Mancini – and not it must be said because he had a hairstyle that looked like it would have cost a woman £100 at a fancy salon. It is an outside shot – given a slight physique – but Meghni could emerge in this tournament and go on to be as famous as Ronaldo, although let's hope not for a silly tuft hairstyle and the best chipmunk impression this side of Santa Cruz de la Sierra.

Coach: Jacques Santini

A Very Quick Quiz

The French National Team includes players born in all of the following except which?

a) Algeria
b) Morocco
c) Kenya
d) Senegal
e) Toulouse

Answers

c) Kenya, as a former British colony. Also, I don't know, because that would take more research than I've got time for, but as rugby playing country, it is also entirely likely that Toulouse does not provide the birth place for any of France's current football squad

Germany:
Rudi Voller

Having played in one of the most impressive German
teams of all time, Rudi Voller has – with the exception of
Michael Ballack – inherited a pretty uninspiring bunch of
players. However, it is a bunch of players he steered to the
World Cup final of 2002. As he now tries to introduce a
new generation of younger players such as Kevin Kuranyi
of Stuttgart, much will depend on Voller's ability to make
the right decisions in allowing Germany to make the best of
what it currently has. So far Voller has been impressive,
and resilient, after the 5-1 mauling by England. Germany
are unlikely to under-perform, it's just a question of
whether the basic talent is currently good enough. Most
Germans think that 2004 is a question of having a team
good enough to win again on home soil in 2006 and that
2004 is going to be won by France.

Ballack will still be the one genuinely world class player
they have. Whilst 'one man team' would be an exaggeration
it must be said that Bayer Leverkusen fell apart without him
and Bayern Munich absolutely strolled the championship of
2002/03 with him. Even playing in a relatively deep
midfield role he got into double figures and continues to
find the net for Germany including as penalty taker. Joining
Ballack on the score-sheet for Germany's last Euro 2004
qualifier against Iceland was young Kevin Kuranyi of
Stuttgart who took advantage of Sean Dundee's injury at

domestic level well enough to earn his call-up to the German national team. He is one of the younger players that Voller wants to have embedded in the national set-up for 2004 and beyond.

Coach: The afore-mentioned Rudi Voller

A Very Quick Quiz

1. Add the minutes to the names!
   a) Owen
   b) Gerrard
   c) Owen
   d) Owen
   e) Heskey
2. Spot the odd minute out: 6, 13, 45, 48, 66, 74.

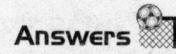

Answers

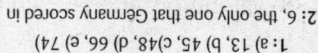

Greece:
Panagiotis Kreonidis

Dubbed the Greek 'Wayne Rooney' this 16-year-old wonder kid – with a Greek father and American mother – has yet to feature in the Olympiakos first team. However, said to possess blistering pace, outstanding vision and a wonderful pair of feet he is the sort of player who dribbles round several players and lashes the ball into the roof of the net with glee. The only problem with Kreonidis, of course, is that he doesn't actually exist. I made him up. But if Greece are to have any chance whatsoever then they had better have a 'Wayne Rooney' up their sleeves somewhere. Sorry Demis Nikolaidis (current top scorer amongst the Greek national squad with 16 in 43 appearances) I just can't see you becoming the surprise name at Euro 2004, although Christos Patsatzoglou might become the unpronounceable name of the tournament.

(Such a pronouncement may seem harsh after the scare Greece gave England in qualifying for Japan/Korea, but that performance must be taken in context. A Greek team long since eliminated playing the best they have for ages against a nervy England. That game was the exception which proves the rule of Greek mediocrity. Of course, there are no easy games in international football – except Germany away – but whilst every team may spring a surprise performance [Paraguay almost knocked France out of the World Cup in 1998 way before the French beat Brazil so easily in the final!] Greece really haven't got the firepower and ability to be classed as a feared team.)

Greece's player of the year in 2002/03 was the player with the name which looks suspiciously like 'limber up a lot' (though what that's got to do with anything I don't know) Nikos Limberopoulos. With a goal every couple of games for Panathinaikos and about one every five games in his 40 caps he is a steady but unspectacular player. Similarly, Anestasios Agritis hasn't had a bad season and at 23 shows a bit of promise. But really, this is an international tournament; not bad, steady and promising will not be enough. Oh Panagiotis Kreonidis wherefore art thou, and when we find you will anyone who knows how to pronounce your name properly?

Coach: Otto Rehhagel

A Very Quick Quiz

Greeks are better at all of the following than they are at football except? (This is a serious-ish question)

a) Weight-lifting
b) Basketball
c) Great food
d) Ancient civilizations
e) Rugby

Answers

e) and let's be fair [and perhaps not as spectacularly as Turkey] Greek football has improved a lot in recent years. I'd certainly bet on them to beat Scotland these days. Despite my harsh words they could yet make me eat humble 'cheese' pie

Holland:
Don't be Ruud, Dick

How they manage to do it is beyond me, but the Dutch just keep churning out players capable of fantastic skill, great goals and accomplished defending. At times the football they play is amazing; as near as Europe is going to get to Brazil and a far, far cry from the neighbouring dour Germans in the park with tyrolean tunics for goal-posts etc. They also seem to have a self-destruct switch which allows them to create arguments at will over topics as important as who's got the best looking missus and whether long hair looks girly.

However, having qualified, whilst the Dutch may prepare for the tournament through pointless recrimination and petty squabbling, by the time they finally step out onto the pitch they are likely to be a big threat. If Ruud Van Nistelrooy plays, his performance in Portugal will be as important as it is in the English Premiership and you wouldn't bet against a renewed battle with Thierry Henry settling this title either. But that's if Ruud can keep at bay not only the competing claims of fellow strikers of exceptional talent (Makaay, Hasselbaink, Kluivert, Van Hooijdonkey etc) but also if he is still talking to them, and/or if the coach is prepared to pick him with certain others who don't like him etc.

Looking to the future, young Wesley Sneijder will barely be out of his teens by the time the group stages finish.

However he has already made a huge impact with Ajax. Like Matthew Le Tissier at Southampton his 'apprenticeship' in the reserves at Ajax was virtually non-existent as he was catapulted into the first team and instantly impressed with his vision. Like the great Saints deity he is also both footed. Of course, this being Holland and not (pre-Sven) England he was quickly playing also for the national team and could emerge in the six months prior to the tournament as the cog which really gets Holland going after they laboured to a 6-1 aggregate play-off victory against Scotland.

Apart from the household names in the squad you could also look out for Andy Van der Meyde and the amusing pronunciation possibilities of Rafael Van Der Vaart and Andre Ooijer. All the others are household names from Van der Sar, through Cocu, Davids, Seedorf, Stam, de Boer etc. If Relate can get involved, or perhaps even Boutros Boutros Ghali, who knows what may be achieved.

Coach: Dick Advocaat

A Very Quick Quiz

Which of the following helps to explain the vicious in-fighting which has characterised the Dutch national football team over the years?

a) relaxed drug laws (contrary to right-wingers' arguments in Britain, this has not led to the falling apart of society, but often a more balanced attitude to drugs, in the context of a much healthier society than we have in Britain)

b) relaxed attitudes to sex (contrary to right-wingers' arguments in Britain, this has not led to raging immorality, but a more responsible attitude to sex amongst the young, in the context of a much lower teenage pregnancy rate than we have in Britain)

c) relaxed licensing laws (contrary to right-wingers' arguments in Britain, this does not mean a permanently drunk population, but a more responsible attitude to drinking, in the context of an enjoyable cafe society)

d) serious environmental legislation (contrary to right-wingers' arguments in Britain, this greater concern for the environment has not damaged the Dutch economy which is still much richer [per person] than ours in Britain)

e) enhanced social benefits (which though not at the levels of Scandinavia still provide the population with a better safety net than we in Britain do for our vulnerable sectors of society)

Answers

Who knows? It's all a bit of a mystery really, isn't it?

Italy:
Christian Vieri

Although the same could be true to a lesser extent of
Filippo Inzaghi, rarely have I been so perplexed by the Vieri
hype one minute, just to see it fully justified the next. The
man clearly has the ability to be awesome. If his pace and
power are put to good effect as he nears his 31st birthday,
Vieri could bow out of international football on a high. As
ever the Italians will look good on paper, and better in the
shirts (as long as you ignore the hair) but the organised
defending and pretty pretty passing must come to
something. Vieri is (possibly) the man, although at the
moment he is sulking his way through matches for
Internazionale, apparently I am told because he wants to
leave. One might be inclined to think he's an ungrateful
rich b******!

As with the Premiership and Ruud Van Nistelrooy, it is
no surprise to learn that last season's player of the year
was a foreigner in Pavel Nedved. However, one player who
has recently emerged is Perugia's Fabrizio Miccoli. So good
that he is now Juventus' Fabrizio Miccoli, he has broken
though into the Azzurri squad at just the right time after
some eye-catching performances. Rumours that previous
elevation to the national squad was thwarted by his refusal
to wear a silly shoulder length wig like the rest of the team
are, of course, absolute twaddle which I just made up.

Coach: Giovanni Trapattoni

A Very Quick Quiz

Azzurri means which of the following:

a) Blues

b) Boys

c) Girls

d) Diving Cheats

e) One of the most over-rated teams in the world, although I'll feel really embarassed about this if they manage to win

Answers

The answer is, of course, 'Blues'

Latvia: Perhaps Miholaps, Perhaps Pahars But Very Definately Verpakovskis

Wow, Latvia seems to have a wealth of attacking talent that no-one has ever heard of. In last season's Latvian championship (2002), Mihail Milohaps won the Latvian golden boot award for a second successive season. Overall he scored a goal a game for Latvian giants Skonto Riga and earned a move to the Russian league for 2003, although like Pahars' move to Southampton he had to settle for a less fashionable club in Spartak-Alaniya. However at international level he has struggled to just a couple of goals at around one every ten games.

For a long time, the goal-scoring responsibilities for Latvia lay on the diminutive shoulders of the little Latvian himself, Marian Pahars. Known as the Latvian Michael Owen, he certainly made the grade at Premiership level after his move from Skonto Riga, taking some of the 'Saints are staying up' duties away from Le Tissier as his powers faded in the late 1990s. However, as Southampton reached the cup final, Pahars moved from one operation to the next, his only real impact on the season being an outrageous dive to take three undeserved points from Everton. At present, rumours of his recovery are much exaggerated or at least each comeback appearance seems to end in a new injury or recurrence of an old one. Him and Agustin Delgado are currently in negotiations to write an article for *The Lancet*, the British medical journal. If he is fit, Latvia will have an attack capable of scoring goals. (At the time of writing Pahars did appear in a Southampton shirt again, looking lively for the last 25 minutes of a 1-0 defeat at Aston Villa. He also played the last two minutes for Latvia against Turkey in the play-off second leg. What the point of that was I'm not sure, but he didn't get injured at least!)

With the inability of Milohaps to click with the national team and Pahars' injuries we have seen the rapid emergence of yet another Skonto Riga player, Maris Verpakovskis. Verpakovskis will no doubt be mispronounced by the so-called experts wheeled out on television, at least unless he does enough to impress them. Turkish commentators already know his name as he scored the only goal of the home leg and one of the Latvia pair in a 2-2 draw as Latvia pleasingly and surprisingly proved that serious surprises are really still possible in international football by winning their play-off against 'third at the World Cup' Turkey. Verpakovskis looks quick and with an eye for goal. Latvian television are calling Michael Owen the old Maris Verpakovskis. Beware.

Verpakovskis finds himself emerging for Latvia in his mid twenties. However, Igor Semjonovs (the Latvian Wayne Rooney?) will not yet be 19 by the time of the tournament. That said, he has emerged as a powerful force in the – you guessed it – Skonto Riga midfield and has already been thrown into the national team. Apart from these players, Latvia doesn't look like it ought to produce surprises, but

the continuing ability of players (eg Kolinko) to perform
beyond their club form will be crucial for what is likely to
become everyone's second team of the tournament.

Coach: Aleksandr Starkovs

A Very Quick Quiz

Which of the following is not a Latvian top division team
who normally trail in after Skonto Riga, who win the title?

a)   Ventspils

b)   Metalurgs

c)   Dinaburg

d)   Valmeira

e)   PFK/Daugava

Answers

e) who withdrew because of financial difficulties

Portugal: The Crowd

Though the 'golden generation' of Portuguese football is felt to have disappointed, the last few years have actually exceeded anything that came before for Portugal in terms of tournament qualification. This time, the remnants of the golden generation have the chance to mix with younger blood and at home too. The talent is undoubted: Figo, Couto, Pauleta, Conceicao, Joao Pinto, Baia not to mention the well hidden potential of Postiga and Boa Morte. There is no doubt this lot can beat the best in the world. In preparation they drew in England and Holland and beat Brazil. As well as the best in the world they also beat Scotland at home. So, much will depend on whether the crowds back them to the hilt, or turn fickle when the chips are down. One suspects that patience is wearing thin amongst the public, so Portugal need to get off to a good start and keep the momentum going; then – like the French public didn't know what football was before 1998 but ended up playing a big part in the success – they may gain the confidence to go on and win it.

Cultural differences are important and should not be mocked, and I can understand, for instance, why the Koreans say the second name before the first name. There's a kind of logic to it which might even be more sensible than the way we do it. But why oh why oh why do Brazilians have just one name? Anyway, one such Brazilian

– now naturalised Portuguese – is Deco. He was player of the season in 2002/03 in which Porto cruised the league, sneaked the cup and broke Celtic hearts in the UEFA Cup (much better to have taken a first round fall and saved your money boys!). In that same season Cristiano Ronaldo presumably did something he no longer does if he was to become one of the hottest properties in Europe. Still, he is still pretty young and perhaps he will perform in a Portugal shirt (what is known as the Smicer effect). Much the same might be said of Helder Posterior.

Coach: Luiz Felipe Scolari

A Very Quick Quiz

If Helder Postiga were not setting the footballing world alight at Tottenham Hotspur, what would he most likely be doing instead?

a)   Reading
b)   Listening to music
c)   Accountancy
d)   A degree in fine art
e)   Fishing

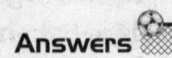

Answers

e) because his father Manuel is a fisherman working out of the Portuguese port of Varzim for whom young Helder played initially

214

Russia:
The Agony of No Choice

Is it just me or do the efficient and dour Soviet teams seem
even more so in the current Russian guise? Looking down
the list of players one struggles to pick out a name which
will set Portugal 2004 alight. Defender Onopko? Forward
Beschastnykh? Midfielder Karpin? Henry the mild-
mannered janitor? Could be! Actually those players have
over 250 caps and 50 international goals between them,
but really I'd probably bet more money on Hong Kong
Phooey setting the European Championships alight.

Leaving aside such cynicism, one name to emerge
recently in domestic soccer is Tajikistan-born Dmitri
Loskov. He scored the decisive goal as Lokomotiv Moscow
beat CSKA Moscow in the play-off match to decide the
2002 title and finally made the national team aged 26.
Despite previous coaches preferring Alexander Mostovoi,
Lostov undoubtedly has talent. An attacking midfielder, he
has the potential to make a big impact in his first major
championships, aged 30. For Russia so far he has not
always done well, but the adjustment from club football
where he has been a central figure may help to explain
that.

Breaking into the Russian team at around the same time
as Loskov was Rotor Volgagrad's Evgeni Aldonin; at 24 he
should have a few more major championships before him
although as a defender – albeit a bit more of a threat than

Claus Lundekvam – he may not have the same potential to become a name as result of the tournament.

Finally, we must forget Alexei Smertin. A player so good and of such proven international class that Roman Abramovich is said to have signed him for Chelsea from Bordeaux as a favour to a business associate (strictly above board all that post-Soviet business dealing right?) but only once they'd found another club mug enough to take him on loan. That club was Portsmouth FC, meaning by default that Smertin is not good enough to have a big impact on Euro 2004.

Coach: Georgi Yartsev

A Very Quick Quiz

Arch 'Ruskie' of the Cold War, Stalin was in fact from which Soviet republic?

a)   Tajikistan
b)   Belarus
c)   Georgia
d)   Latvia
e)   Estonia

Answers

c) Georgia

Spain: Raul, Finally? Or Will Reyes be King of Kings?

We can, if we want, rabbit on about 30 years (and rising) of hurt and all that, but imagine being a Spanish football supporter. Chances are you may have stronger local allegiances in the first place, but in any case, watching your team under-perform must have been cruel torture year after year. And imagine that in 1966, if instead of England winning the thing we had struggled to a 1-1 draw with Honduras and lost 1-0 at home to Northern Ireland before limply getting eliminated. So what hope this time for Spain, who did just this in 1982? Which of the big names might finally remember to produce the performance the stage demands?

Well it seems almost silly to talk about the established stars. We all know they are capable of almost anything, including losing 1-0 at home to Greece and making probably the most spectacular cock up ever by a team playing in a major championships as hosts. So let us forget the superstars of Spanish football of the past and talk instead of Jose Antonio Reyes. I don't know if you remember, but back in late 2003 the Real Madrid coach Carlos Quieros – after extensive lessons on being irritating from Alex Ferguson whilst at Man U – responded to suggestions that Real Madrid needed a top quality defender by saying that his team of superstars did not need defenders because they attacked and therefore did not need to defend. Do you remember that?

Well, the next game was against Sevilla. After about 30 minutes the score was Sevilla 4-0 Real Madrid with the home team ultimately cruising to a 4-1 victory. By that time Madrid had withdrawn a young defender – I forget his name – whose performance had been similar to the rest of the 'defence', but he was made the scapegoat. He sat on the bench sobbing. I sent him a video of Scott Marshall – allegedly decribed by Francis Benali as the worst player he'd ever seen – to cheer him up a bit (I must remember to send Francis a video of himself). In any case, in that spell where Sevilla went 4-0 up, it was not simply the quality of Madrid's defending which was their downfall, but that Jose Antonio Reyes absolutely took them apart.

World Soccer recently described the 20-year-old as a 'fantasy footballer', and certainly he looks to have pace, skill and vision in abundance. Like others with such talent he seemed occasionally to exasperate his manager at Sevilla, although he must have been pleased to have such a quality player in a team renowned for no-nonsense toughness and hard tackling. Unfortunately for him, Arsene Wengor was also pleased with Reyes' performances, so much so that he forked out Arsenal's record fee – £17m – to bring him over to Highbury. Reyes has recently been promoted to the Spanish national team. He seems full of confidence, and with the play-offs out of the way, maybe he is the player that can encourage Spain finally to fulfil their potential.

Coach: Inaki Saez

A Very Quick Quiz

Which is the nastiest 'derby' game in the world?

- a) Lazio-Roma
- b) Southampton-Portsmouth
- c) River-Boca
- d) Betis-Sevilla
- e) Blackburn-Burnley

Sweden:
Anders Svensson

Talking of patience wearing thin (as in Spanish fans and
their team)...come on Anders...what's it all about eh? You
bang in the free-kicks versus Argentina, you almost win the
game with a golden goal against Senegal with the most
fantastic drag back and shot. Every time I look at a Swedish
score you seem to have scored or been involved and
you're averaging a goal every four games from midfield.

Answers

Having only experienced one of them I really can't say, but the Seville derby is renowned for
its passion. Betis president Manuel Ruiz de Lopera recently forbade his players from
'fraternising' with any of Sevilla's for instance.

And yet put you in a Saints shirt! You need an extra touch, you don't seem to put your foot in and you score one goal every eight games (and rising). Come on man! You look lazy and lethargic and the fact that you were supposed to be the creative replacement for Le Tiss is no excuse. Sort it out! Go and wow them in Portugal and then come back and start knocking them in for the Saints (although if his form gets any lower I wouldn't bank on him being with the Saints by then). The other Svensson from Southampton might also be important.

Worth mentioning in amongst all the Svenssons, Anderssons and such like are Niklas Skoog and Dick Last. No idea what their football is like (Last has only one cap) but great names. Actually Skoog has four goals in four games though all against Qatar and North Korea so don't hold your breath any.

To be taken more seriously, as any sportsman called Kim really should be, is Kim Kallstrom, one important reason why Djurgardens won the Swedish league in 2002 (a title they retained in 2003). A strong two-footed midfielder who gets his fair share of goals...hey, maybe they'd swap him for Anders. Kallstrom is only young so could emerge at Portugal 2004. Alexander Farnerud is a couple of years younger than Kallstrom but is already a target of many clubs. He has already played for and scored for the national team.

Coaches: The very wonderfully-named Lars Lagerback and Tommy Soderberg

A Very Quick Quiz

Which is the funniest joke?
a)   The Swedish chemist sketch in which the man wants to buy a deodorant and for which the punchline is 'Neither, I want it for my armpits'
b)   The joke about why does a dog lick its balls told in Norwegian
c)   The joke about why no one goes hungry in the desert

Switzerland:
Alexander Frei

Alexander Frei is 24 years old and plays in Rennes with the Czech goalie chap (Cech)...at least until Cech departs for Chelski. Frei is scoring a goal every one and a half games for Switzerland and will need to take the majority of chances coming his way if they are to produce any surprises this time. Let's face it the Swiss will need something. This is not to under-estimate a side which drew

Answers

c) with the totally amusing punchline being; 'Because of all the sandwiches there'...sand which is there...geddit?

221

with the hosts in both World Cup USA 94 and Euro 96 but, and this is a big but (as the Archbishop of Canterbury said to the Duchess of York) something really special will need to emerge for them.

In this sense, one wonders if the European Under-17 Championship-winning team of 2002 offers any promise for the Swiss. Yes and no. Of course by 2006, 2008 and 2010 this group of players may have produced several fine players for the Swiss national team. However, in the short term the best of those players is Phillippe Senderos. The 'however' in that last sentence says nothing about my feelings concerning Senderos' obvious potential and everything about the fact that he is a defender which may not be where Switzerland need the talent to emerge. Furthermore, it is by no means certain that at just 17 young Phillippe has time in any case to break into the national team by the summer of 2004.

Coach: Kobi Kuhn

A Very Quick Quiz

Several languages, cuckoo clocks, mountains, cheese full of holes, expensive everything, yodelling, refusal to join the UN, let alone the EU. How are we to characterise the Swiss?

a) Odd
b) Distinctly odd
c) Strange
d) Very strange
e) Barking

Conclusion

The schedule of tournament matches below throws up some intriguing possibilities, and aside from England's involvement in the tournament we are sure to see some great games. As well as our own historical rivalry with the French, the draw also throws up matches between traditional and ancient enemies. Thus the Danes meet the Swedes, Germany play both Czechs and Dutch (neither of whom are especially fond of them) and the hosts Portugal take on their Iberian neighbours Spain.

Answers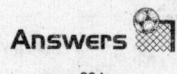

Yes

Here is a list of the matches, times etc with a little information to follow on the venues themselves.

Schedule of Tournament Matches

Group/Match Number	Game
A	Portugal/Greece
A	Spain/Russia
B	Switzerland/Croatia
B	France/England
C	Denmark/Italy
C	Sweden/Bulgaria
D	Czech Republic/Latvia
D	Germany/Holland
A	Greece/Spain
A	Russia/Portugal
B	England/Switzerland
B	Croatia/France
C	Bulgaria/Denmark
C	Italy/Sweden
D	Latvia/Germany

Time (UK)/Date	Venue	Score (tbc)
5pm/12/06	Oporto	
7.45pm/12/06	Faro-Loule	
5pm/13/06	Leiria	
7.45pm/13/06	Lisbon	
5pm/14/06	Guimaraes	
7.45pm/14/06	Lisbon	
5pm/15/06	Aveiro	
7.45pm/15/06	Porto	
5pm/16/06	Porto	
7.45pm/16/06	Lisbon	
5pm/17/06	Coimbra	
7.45pm/17/06	Leiria	
5pm/18/06	Braga	
7.45pm/18/06	Porto	
5pm/19/06	Porto	

Group/Match Number	Game
D	Holland/CzechRepublic
A	Spain/Portugal
A	Russia/Greece
B	Croatia/England
B	Switzerland/France
C	Italy/Bulgaria
C	Denmark/Sweden
D	Holland/Latvia
D	Germany/Czech Rep
25	Winner Group A v Runner Up Group B
26	Winner Group B v Runner Up Group A
27	Winner Group C v Runner Up Group D
28	Winner Group D v Runner Up Group C
29	Winner Match 25 v Winner Match 27
30	Winner Match 26 v Winner Match 28
FINAL	Winner Match 29 v Winner Match 30

Time (UK)/Date	Venue	Score (tbc)
7.45pm/19/06	Aveiro	
7.45pm/20/06	Lisbon	
7.45pm/20/06	Faro-Loule	
7.45pm/21/06	Lisbon	
7.45pm/21/06	Coimbra	
7.45pm/22/06	Guimaraes	
7.45pm/22/06	Porto	
7.45pm/23/06	Braga	
7.45pm/23/06	Lisbon	
7.45pm/24/06	Lisbon	
7.45/25/06	Lisbon	
7.45pm/26/06	Faro-Loule	
7.45pm/27/06	Porto	
7.45pm/30/06	Lisbon	
7.45pm/01/07	Porto	
7.45pm/04/07	Lisbon	

Of the 10 stadia which will be used in the finals, seven have the minimum tournament capacity of 30,000. Only the Dragao in Oporto and the Jose Alvalade (52,000) and Da Luz (where the final will be held on 4 July, 65,000) in Lisbon hold more. Portugal has invested nearly £300 million in hosting the tournament including 10 stadia of which seven will have been built completely from scratch. As outsiders to host the tournament in the first place, many suggested that Portugal would not be up to the task (predicting chaos and incompetence in organisation) and domestically the suggestion has been that the money would have been better spent on helping resolve social problems and that the expense will simply place even further burdens on an already creaking Portuguese economy. Of course the hope is that despite a considerable investment, tourism will massively increase thus partially, or even wholly, paying for the tournament and attracting to Portugal people who may never have been before but might subsequently revisit. Furthermore, the venues have attracted more Portuguese fans for the current season.

Alphabetical Listing of the Venues

Aveiro

They'll be just two group matches at this stadium especially built for the tournament. It holds 30,000 fans and the team of Beira Mar. It is one of three stadia with the magical 'Municipal' label as its name.

Braga

Like the Municipal at Aveiro, this is a newly constructed stadium for 30,000 fans which will host two group games and is called Estadio Municipal. The home team is called Sporting Braga. I'm sure 'braga' in Spanish has something to do with ladies' underwear, although why that is relevant here God alone knows.

Coimbra

This is one of the 'remodelled' stadia, in Portugal's former historic capital, extending to 30,000 the capacity for home team Academica (in a city most famous for its university, with ancient traditions). Again the stadium is a municipal one and again two group games will take place here.

Faro-Loule

A brand new stadium on the Algarve with lovely wave-like patterns on the seats. It will host two group matches and one quarter-final. Called the Estadio Algarve.

Guimaraes

The attractive Estadio Afonso Henriques has been remodelled to hold the minimum required 30,000. Normally playing here are Vitoria Guimaraes, the sort of team that serious 'anoraks' have heard of but not normal people. There will be two group matches here.

Leiria

Not for Leiria the Municipal tag. No the home stadium for Uniao Leiria – which will host two group matches – is called Dr Magalhaes Pessoa, possibly after the most famous Portuguese writer of recent times, although I'm not sure and haven't got time to check! Capacity has been increased from a modest 11,000 to 30,000.

Lisbon (Benfica)

A brand new Estadio da Luz has been built next to the old one, and the remarkable space age-construction holds 65,000. Benfica's ground is going to host five matches in total including the final. The stadium has the technology to go with the space-age look. Behind each goal are a couple of dozen internet connections allowing pictures to be relayed instantly. There are 1,000 press places and over 100 commentary positions.

Lisbon (Sporting)

The new Estadio Jose Alvalade has a capacity of 52,000 which Sporting are now half-filling on a regular basis as Portuguese fans begin to get enthusiastic about the championships. The old Estadio Jose Alvalade (next door) was getting average crowds of less than 10,000. Three group games, a quarter and a semi-final will be here.

Oporto (FC Porto)

Like the Lisbon variety, the new Estadio Dragao has been thrown up next to the old Estadio das Antas. Like the Estadio Jose Alvalade it holds 52,000 spectators. The home of FC Porto it will host the tournament's opening game, two other group matches, a quarter-final and a semi-final. Estadio Dragao probably means Dragon Stadium. Estadio das Antas is less likely to mean Stadium of Ants but you never can tell.

Oporto (Boavista)

The Estadio do Bessa has been rebuilt for the championships with several extra seating sections. The home of Boavista will host three group matches and holds, like all but three of the tournament stadia, 30,000 spectators.

Predictions

After the success you have already witnessed in terms of my ability to predict the play-offs (Latvia have got no chance, Slovenia will be shock winners etc) I thought I'd have another go and invite you to see if you can do any better. In terms of my post-tournament reputation, what I have done is produce two different books for the tournament and in this one I actually make different predictions from the other one to double my chances! Anyway, the scoring works like this.

You get three points for the correct score. Thus if you predict Sweden 2-2 Denmark and it is 2-2 you get three points.

You get one point for the correct result. Thus is you predicted 2-2 but it turns out to be Sweden 1-1 Denmark you get one point. You get nothing for 3-2 even if it was a hotly disputed last-minute penalty and you feel cheated.

You get double points if you predict the team <u>not</u> in capital letters to win and they do (i.e. the underdogs). For example, let's take France v England as an example. France are the favourites (in my opinion – it's my scoring system) so the match appears thus:

FRANCE v England

This is what you should already know from the above:
If you predict France to win 1-0 and they do, you get three points.
If you predict France to win 1-0 and they win 2-1 (for example) you get one point.
If you predict a 1-1 draw and it is, you get three points.
If you predict a 1-1 draw and it's 2-2 you get one point.

BUT:

If you predict England to win 1-0 and they do, because you have predicted the underdogs to win you get double points. For the exact score that would be six points. If England won by a different score you would get two points (i.e. 2 x 1). Does that make sense?

There's bound to be some shocks and this system helps reward you for spotting them. OK, so here we go. The matches, my prediction and a space for you to enter my points and your points. (Sometimes the favourites will only be marginal – or you may disagree – but we're all playing to the same rules! You also have the advantage of not making your predictions on a cold December day…unless it's December 2004, in which case you're cheating!)

And the Winner Is…

Well almost certainly me, but let's just check shall we?

Group	My Points	Your Points
Group A		
Group B		
Group C		
Group D		
Grand Totals		

Group A				
Match	My Prediction	My Points	Your Prediction	Your Points
PORTUGAL v Greece	2-0		3-0	
SPAIN v Russia	3-1		2-0	
Greece v SPAIN	0-4		0-2	
Russia v PORTUGAL	1-4		1-2	
Spain v PORTUGAL	1-0		1-1	
RUSSIA v Greece	2-0		0-0	
Total Points				

Group B				
Match	My Prediction	My Points	Your Prediction	Your Points
Switzerland v CROATIA	2-1		0-1	
FRANCE v England	2-2		1-0	
ENGLAND v Switzerland	1-0		2-1	
Croatia v FRANCE	1-2		1-2	
Croatia v ENGLAND	0-2		1-2	
Switzerland v FRANCE	0-3		0-3	
Total Points				

Match	My Prediction	My Points	Your Prediction	Your Points
Denmark v ITALY	1-2		0 - 1	
SWEDEN v Bulgaria	1-1		2 - 1	
Bulgaria v DENMARK	1-1		1 - 1	
ITALY v Sweden	1-1		1 - 0	
ITALY v Bulgaria	3-1		2 - 0	
Denmark v SWEDEN	0-2		0 - 1	
Total Points				

Group C

Group D				
Match	My Prediction	My Points	Your Prediction	Your Points
CZECH REPUBLIC v Latvia	0-0		2-0	
GERMANY v Holland	0-2		1-1	
Latvia v GERMANY	0-0		0-2	
Holland v CZECH REPUBLIC	1-2		2-2	
HOLLAND v Latvia	3-1		2-0	
GERMANY v Czech Republic	2-2		1-1	
Total Points				

Further Predictions

Well I am almost certain to have got those predictions wrong, but if I am right, the quarter-finalists would be: Spain, Portugal, England, France, Italy, Sweden, Holland and Czech Republic. I cannot see too many problems with this, although it does fall into the trap of writing off the Germans, who would probably expect to qualify instead of either the Czechs or Dutch.

However as we saw at the World Cup where both Argentina and France went out at the group stage despite being pre-tournament favourites, anything can happen. That said, Group A looks easiest to predict with Spain and Portugal streets ahead. In group B either Switzerland or Croatia will hope to oust either France, or more likely given their European record, England, for one of the two places. Group C looks the closest to being a 'group of death' with Denmark and Bulgaria looking like tough opposition for Sweden and Italy. Finally Group D where it really is any two from three. Everyone will want Latvia to do it again, but they might just be happy to be at the party this time around.

If you press me to predict the final, it goes something like this (dream, dream, dream...). England's run to the final is not wholly impressive. Much of the burden, especially in terms of goal-scoring, falls to David Beckham in the form of penalties and free-kicks in and around the box. In Australia the whinging Matilda newspapers bemoan the dominance of English sport in the world. In France *L'Equipe* runs a feature on England's opening game draw with France. England barely get out of their own half, pegged back by free-flowing French football, and only kept in the game by Beckham's tireless running, accurate passing to the front men outlets and tenacious tackling. England's equalising goal in that game was scored in injury time from a long-distance free-kick from Beckham (the first was a rather fortunate goal-mouth scramble which bounces in off Makalele from a Terry header). So *L'Equipe* have a picture of Beckham under the heading 'Est-ce que c'est tout que vous avez'. (Is that all that you've got?)

Further French taunting accompanies England's route to the final. The 1-0 against the Swiss comes courtesy of a penalty, and the fortunate 2-0 win against Croatia which put England through to the quarter-finals was completely against the run of play. Whilst the semi-final win against Portugal was always likely to be a case of hitting a passionately backed opponent on the break (Rooney and Owen chipping in) it was once again settled by a Beckham free-kick and the French mocked and boasted of how they would turn us over in the final.

Indeed, in the early stages it looked like they would do just that, scoring after just five minutes through Henry. But back came England through a penalty and then a move of exquisite pace and passing, finished off by a thunderous Lampard volley giving the lie to England only being able to score from set-pieces. In the second half, France seemed to get all the dodgy refereeing decisions and gradually took control. Just when it seemed England would escape, Terry (in for the disgraced Rio Ferdinand) mis-controlled on the edge of his own box and gave away a free-kick in trying to recover. Henry blasted home with just seconds to go. And so to extra time, the match went to and fro, but with just 19 seconds left Beckham's half-volley flew into the corner of the net. 'Est-ce que c'est tout que vous avez' indeed!

England win 3-2. My wife calls this kind of 'if only' story telling 'football w***ing'! (Of course it doesn't sound anything like the

rugby World Cup final adapted to football!). But dreams can
come true...and you know you've got to have one.

And Finally

If you do go to Portugal beware of driving and Brazilian
prostitutes. Be nice to policemen and learn enough Portuguese
to say hello and thanks. Don't drink too quickly and remember to
pack enough clean underwear. Here is a handy guide to pertinent
phrases:

Thank you – Obrigado/a (o for men, a for women)
Aye – Sim
Nay – Nao
Hiya – Bom dia
Oh go on – por favor
Do you speak English? – Fala ingles?
Sorry mate, I ain't go a clue what yer on about – Nao percebo
Way in – entrada
Exit – Saida

None of the above include authentic accents, but let's face it, if
you don't speak Portuguese, like what I don't, then you're not
going to pronounce it properly anyway. And if like me you're
going to save the money and sit in front of your telly with a bottle
of Port or Mateus Rose to get yourself in the mood...enjoy!
And c'mon England!